National 4 & 5

History

Changing Britain 1760–1900

John A. Kerr

HODDER
GIBSON
AN HACHETTE UK COMPANY

The Publishers would like to thank the following for permission to reproduce copyright material:

Photo credits: **p.2** Getty Images; **p.3** RIA Novosti/Topfoto; **p.12** (top) Mary Evans Picture Library, (bottom) Amoret Tanner/ Alamy; **p.15** Time & Life Pictures/Getty Images; **p.18** Mary Evans Picture Library/CHARLES COULDRY; **p.19** ALAN OLIVER/Alamy; **p.23** Fine Art Images/Heritage Images/Topfoto; **p.24** The Granger Collection/Topfoto; **p.26** (top) British Library Board/Robana/Topfoto, (bottom) The Granger Collection/Topfoto; **p.27** (bottom) The Granger Collection/Topfoto; **p.29** The Granger Collection/Topfoto; **p.31** SSPL via Getty Images; **p.35** (left) British Library Board/Robana/Topfoto, (right) World History Archive/Topfoto; **p.37** The Granger Collection/Topfoto; **p.38** (top and bottom) The Granger Collection/ Topfoto; **p.39** Private Collection/© Look and Learn/The Bridgeman Art Library; **pp.40, 42** © New Lanark Trust. Licensor www.scran.ac.uk; **p.48** Topfoto; **p.50** (top) World History Archive/Topfoto, (bottom left and bottom right) Classic Image/ Alamy; **p.51** (top) The Granger Collection/Topfoto, (bottom) Oldtime/Alamy; **p.53** (top) Mary Evans Picture Library/ Alamy; **p.56** Mary Evans Picture Library/Alamy; **p.60** HIP/Topfoto; **p.63** SSPL via Getty Images; **p.64** Anthony Collins/ Alamy; **p.65** Image by courtesy of the Wedgwood Museum, Barlaston, Staffordshire, UK; **p.67** David Hoffman Photo Library/Alamy; **p.68** Juice Images/Alamy; **p.71** Private Collection/© Look and Learn/The Bridgeman Art Library; **p.72** liszt collection/Alamy; **p.73** INTERFOTO/Alamy; **p.74** The Art Archive/Alamy; **p.75** © CSG CIC Glasgow Museums Collection; **p.76** World History Archive/Topfoto; **p.78** (top and bottom) Science and Society/SuperStock; **p.79** Science and Society/ SuperStock; **p.81** Reproduced by permission of Durham University Library/DUL NSR Planfile C 22/5; **p.84** The Granger Collection/Topfoto; **p.85** Mary Evans Picture Library/Alamy; **p.87** Topham Picturepoint; **p.88** World History Archive/ Topfoto; **p.89** (top) Image Copyright kim traynor. This work is licensed under the Creative Commons Attribution-Share Alike 2.0 Generic Licence. To view a copy of this licence, visit http://creativecommons.org/licenses/by-sa/2.0/or send a letter to Creative Commons, 171 Second Street, Suite 300, San Francisco, California, 94105, USA, (bottom) Niall Ferguson/ Alamy; **p.90** Image Copyright Lairich Rig. This work is licensed under the Creative Commons Attribution-Share Alike 2.0 Generic Licence. To view a copy of this licence, visit http://creativecommons.org/licenses/by-sa/2.0/or send a letter to Creative Commons, 171 Second Street, Suite 300, San Francisco, California, 94105, USA; **p.93** British Library Board. All Rights Reserved/The Bridgeman Art Library; **p.95** Mary Evans Picture Library; **p.96** Private Collection/The Bridgeman Art Library; **p.97** Getty Images; **p.98** Liszt Collection/Topfoto; **p.99** © The Trustees of the British Museum; **p.102** Mary Evans Picture Library; **p.103** World History Archive/Topfoto; **p.104** (top) © Punch Limited, (bottom) Anthony Morgan/Alamy. With kind permission of Budd Mosaics; **p.105** (top) Royal Collection Trust/© Her Majesty Queen Elizabeth II 2013; **p.106** Punch Limited/Topfoto; **p.110** (top) HIP/Topfoto, (bottom) The Granger Collection/Topfoto; **p.111** Mary Evans Picture Library/ Alamy; **p.113** Topfoto/HIP.

Although every effort has been made to ensure that website addresses are correct at time of going to press, Hodder Gibson cannot be held responsible for the content of any website mentioned in this book. It is sometimes possible to find a relocated web page by typing in the address of the home page for a website in the URL window of your browser.

Hachette UK's policy is to use papers that are natural, renewable and recyclable products and made from wood grown in sustainable forests. The logging and manufacturing processes are expected to conform to the environmental regulations of the country of origin.

Orders: please contact Bookpoint Ltd, 130 Park Drive, Abingdon, Oxon OX14 4SE. Telephone: (44) 01235 827720. Fax: (44) 01235 400454. Lines are open 9.00–5.00, Monday to Saturday, with a 24-hour message answering service. Visit our website at www.hoddereducation.co.uk. Hodder Gibson can be contacted direct on: Tel: 0141 848 1609; Fax: 0141 889 6315; email: hoddergibson@hodder.co.uk

First published in 2014 by
Hodder Gibson, an imprint of Hodder Education,
An Hachette UK Company
2a Christie Street
Paisley PA1 1NB

Impression number	5	4	3	2	1	
Year	2018	2017	2016	2015	2014	

Cover photo © RCAHMS (Scottish Colorfoto Collection). Licensor www.rcahms.gov.uk
Illustrations by Gray Publishing
Produced and typeset in 10/11pt Folio Light by Gray Publishing, Tunbridge Wells
Printed in Italy

A catalogue record for this title is available from the British Library

ISBN: 978 1444 187 175

Contents

Preface

This is one of a series of six titles for the National 4 & 5 History courses to be assessed from 2014 onwards. Students should study three main units in National 4 & 5 History, with a very wide selection of topics to choose from (five in the first two, ten in the third). This series covers two topics in each unit.

The six titles in the series are:

▶ National 4 & 5 History: Migration and Empire 1830–1939
▶ National 4 & 5 History: The Era of the Great War 1910–1928
▶ National 4 & 5 History: The Atlantic Slave Trade 1770–1807
▶ National 4 & 5 History: Changing Britain 1760–1900
▶ National 4 & 5 History: Hitler and Nazi Germany 1919–1939
▶ National 4 & 5 History: Free at Last? Civil Rights in the USA 1918–1968

Each book will contain comprehensive coverage of the four areas of mandatory content for National 5 as well as guidance and practice on assignment writing and assessment procedures.

The Assignment: what you need to know

National 5

What is the Assignment for National 5?

The Assignment is written under exam conditions and then sent to the SQA to be marked. It counts for 20 marks out of a total of 80, so doing well in the Assignment can provide you with a very useful launchpad for overall success in the National 5 exam.

What can I write about?

You can write about a question linked to this book or something from another section in the course. In fact, you can write about any historical topic you want. You can even do your Assignment on local history.

What should I write about?

If you decide to do an Assignment based on the content of this book, here are some *good* possible questions:

✓ Why was health and housing such a problem in nineteenth-century cities?
✓ To what extent did technology and laws help to improve working conditions in textile mills between 1760 and 1900?
✓ Is it true to say that coalmining got safer but was never safe between 1760 and 1900?
✓ Which had a greater effect on Britain between 1760 and 1900: canals or railways?
✓ How important were protest organisations in helping to make Britain more democratic?
✓ To what extent did Britain become more democratic between 1760 and 1900?

What follows are *bad* titles for an Assignment:

✗ Problems with health and housing in Britain.
✗ Working in coal mines and cotton mills.
✗ The growth of canals.
✗ Railways and change in Britain.
✗ The Radicals.
✗ Changes in democracy in Britain between 1760 and 1900.

Be safe! There are no prizes for giving yourself a difficult question that you have made up yourself.

Choose something from the history you have already been studying.

Avoid doing something risky – you only get one chance at this Assignment.

How long should my Assignment be?

Your Assignment has no set length – it is what you can write in 1 hour. Most Assignments are about four or five pages long.

What skills must I show I am using to get a good mark?

- You must choose a question to write about. That means your title should end with a question mark. Don't just write a heading down because you will just start writing a story or a project. Your teacher is allowed to give you a little help with making your choice of title.
- Collect relevant evidence from *at least* two sources of information. For example, these could be two books or one book plus an interview.
- Organise and use your information to help answer your question.
- Use your own knowledge and understanding to answer the question that you have chosen.
- Include *at least* two different points of view about your question in your answer.
- Write a conclusion that sums up your information and ends up by answering the question you started with.

Remember that you also have a Resource Sheet to help you

On your Resource Sheet you will write out the sources that you will refer to in your Assignment. This will show the marker that you have researched, selected and organised your information.

Your Resource Sheet will be sent to the SQA with your finished Assignment. You will not be given a mark for your completed Resource Sheet but markers will use it to see that you have done the necessary research and have found appropriate sources to use in your Assignment. There is no time limit for completing your Resource Sheet and no word count. The Resource Sheet is *yours*. You can change it, colour it or print it out. You can write it anywhere, anytime before you write your Assignment under exam conditions.

National 4: Added Value Unit

The Assignment lets you show off your skills as you research a historical issue. You have a lot of choice in what you can find out about and you can also choose to present your findings in different ways. That means you don't have to create a long written response to display your skills, knowledge and understanding.

To be successful in National 4 you have to show you can research and use information by doing the following things:

- Choosing an appropriate historical theme or event for study. Your teacher can help you choose.
- Collecting relevant evidence from *at least two* sources of information.
- Organising and using the information that you have collected to help you write about the subject you have chosen.
- Describing what your chosen subject is about.
- Explaining why your chosen subject happened (its cause) or explaining what happened next because of your chosen subject (its effects).

As you work through this book you will make mobiles, give presentations, and create posters and artwork. All these things could be part of your National 4 Assignment. You then have to present your findings.

Don't worry – if you get stuck your teacher is allowed to give you help and advice at *any* stage as you do your Assignment.

Do I have to write a long essay?

No, you don't. You can choose how you present your Assignment. You could do a talk and then be asked some questions about your subject by your teacher. You could do a PowerPoint presentation or keep a learning log or design a poster or some other way to display your work. You could even submit a long written response if you wanted to!

Chapter 1 Introduction

What is this course about?

This course is about how Britain changed into a modern industrial country between 1760 and 1900. The book looks at these changes and how they affected people all over Britain, sometimes in a good way and sometimes not. It is about how people's lives were transformed by forces beyond their control and it is also about how people struggled to regain control over their lives.

What will this book help me to do?

This book will help you to be successful in your National 5 and 4 History course. It contains everything you need to know about all the mandatory content and illustrative examples provided by the SQA for 'Changing Britain 1760–1900'.

The book provides advice and examples to help you to answer all the different types of questions you are likely to face in the National 5 exam.

Finally, this book will provide guidance to help you work on the Added Value Assignment tasks.

Additional resources

Find out more about how Britain changed between 1760 and 1900:

- http://en.wikipedia.org/wiki/Life_in_Great_Britain_during_the_Industrial_Revolution
- www.nationalarchives.gov.uk/education/victorianbritain/default.htm
- www.victorianweb.org/technology/railways/railway4.html
- www.nationalarchives.gov.uk/education/lesson13.htm
- www.nationalarchives.gov.uk/education/lessons/lesson14.htm

What caused such big changes?

The main force causing change beyond the control of ordinary people was **industrialisation**. When industrialisation was happening there were changes in the way people worked, lived and even travelled. Instead of people working in their own houses and villages, they worked more and more in **factories**.

Traditionally, items had been made by hand; now all sorts of things were being made by machine. People who had lived more or less in the same village all their lives, now began to travel further and faster.

A word for a big change is revolution. The big changes caused by industrialisation meant that this time of change was called the **Industrial Revolution**.

Look at the pictures of the opening ceremony of the London Olympics in 2012 below and on page 3. You can also find the relevant part of the opening ceremony on YouTube.

The opening ceremony of the 2012 Olympics tried to give an impression of what life in Britain was like around 1750, just before the Industrial Revolution.

The opening ceremony of the 2012 Olympics also tried to give an impression of what life in Britain was like in 1850, while the Industrial Revolution was happening.

Activity 1

▶ Work in groups of three or four. One of your group must be a recorder who writes down what people say. Each member of the group should take a turn to suggest two adjectives (describing words) which tell you what life was like in Britain around 1760, based on what you see in the photograph on page 2. Keep going until your group has at least 20 words.

▶ Do the same task again, but this time based on the photograph at the top of this page.

Activity 2

In your workbook or work file draw a table with two columns. One column should have the heading 'Social change'. (Social change means changes to how people lived their lives.)

The second column should have the heading 'Economic change'. (Economic change means changes to how and where people worked and changes to businesses and transport.)

Compare the two photographs on pages 2 and 3. In each column of your table write down as many changes as you can see that happened between 1750 and 1850. Now add things to your columns that you can guess or infer must be happening in Britain because of what you can see in the second photograph.

Activity 3

The photographs you have looked at indicate some of the effects of industrialisation. From looking at the photographs and thinking about the main word 'industry', in your own words try to explain your ideas of what industrialisation means.

Chapter 2 The growing population

What is this chapter about?

Between 1760 and 1900 the British population grew quickly and the change in the population had big effects on life in Britain. Every year there were more mouths to feed, and towns and cities grew as people moved there looking for work. This led to more people searching for housing and that in turn caused overcrowding and health problems. This chapter looks at why the population grew so fast and if this was a cause or an effect of industrialisation.

By the end of this chapter you should be able to:

▶ Describe some of the effects of the growing population.
▶ Explain why the population of Britain grew so quickly after 1760.

The chicken and the egg

It's an old question that has no final answer: which came first, the chicken or the egg? The chicken clearly laid the egg, but the chicken must have hatched out of an egg. The same round and round sort of argument can happen with the issue of population growth and change. Did the population of Britain change because of industrialisation, or did industrialisation lead to a growth in population? The answer is a bit of both.

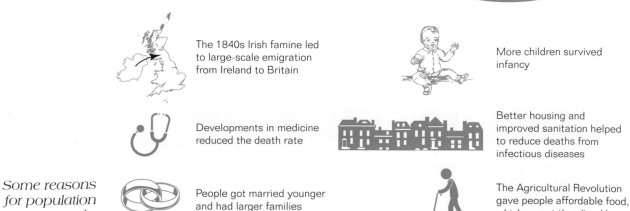

The 1840s Irish famine led to large-scale emigration from Ireland to Britain

More children survived infancy

Developments in medicine reduced the death rate

Better housing and improved sanitation helped to reduce deaths from infectious diseases

Some reasons for population growth.

People got married younger and had larger families

The Agricultural Revolution gave people affordable food, which meant they lived longer

How do we know about the size of the population?

We can find out about growth in population using national records. Since 1801, the British government has taken a census. This is when the government tries to count the number of people in the country on a certain day ('census day'). A census takes place every ten years. The census is a very reliable, detailed and accurate source of information.

The census is a list of questions about the people who live in Britain. To begin with, the census asked only a few simple questions, but after 1841 there were more questions to answer. These included questions about a person's place of birth, their job, if they were married and so on. In Scotland, the first attempt at an accurate count of the population was made in 1755 by the Reverend Alexander Webster, who calculated that Scotland at that time contained 1,265,380 people.

In words, describe what happened to the population of the UK between 1801 and 1901. Remember that all of Ireland was part of the UK until the 1920s.

Census	England and Wales	Scotland	Ireland
1801	8,893,000	1,608,000	Not available
1821	12,000,000	2,092,000	6,802,000
1841	15,914,000	2,620,000	8,178,000
1861	20,066,000	3,062,000	5,799,000
1881	25,974,000	3,736,000	5,175,000
1901	32,528,000	4,472,000	4,459,000

Population of the UK from 1801 to 1901.

Activity 1

Numeracy counts

▶ Roughly, by how many times did the population of England and Wales increase between 1801 and 1901?
▶ Roughly, by how many times did the population of Scotland increase between 1801 and 1901?
▶ What is odd about the Irish statistics after 1841? Can you suggest any reasons for the **anomaly** of the Irish statistics?
▶ Convert the statistics in the table into either a colourful bar chart or a line graph to show the population changes of England and Wales, Scotland and Ireland between 1801 and 1901.

GLOSSARY

Anomaly something odd that does not fit into a pattern. It stands out as different

Why did the population of Britain grow so quickly after 1760?

The main cause of population growth before 1870 was the increase in the birth rate. That means that more babies were being born than there were people dying. Later in the nineteenth century the death rate fell. With fewer people dying at an earlier age and larger numbers of children surviving past infancy, there were more people alive. Many of those people became parents themselves and so even more people were born. However, to say the death rate fell and birth rate rose just leads to other questions, such as why did the birth and death rates change?

Industrialisation had an effect

As more factories opened, more workers were needed. The larger population needed things such as clothes and everyday items, and this meant that more of these things had to be made. Inventors had an **incentive** to come up with more efficient ways of producing what people needed and wanted. Some of the first inventions increased the production of cotton clothing.

The old way of making things was called the domestic system, because things were made in people's homes. The new way of working was based in factories and those factories provided employment for people. The availability of factory jobs meant that couples could earn enough to get married at a younger age and start families, so the population increased even more.

> **GLOSSARY**
>
> **Incentive** a reason for doing something
>
> **Medical advances** improvements in medical knowledge
>
> **Agricultural Revolution** agricultural means things to do with farming; revolution means a big change

Medical knowledge improved

Before 1850, doctors did not know much about what caused diseases and they could do little to prevent or cure illnesses. After 1850, there were significant **medical advances**; Joseph Lister invented antiseptics and the work of Louis Pasteur and Robert Koch led to the discovery that bacteria caused and spread disease.

In London, Dr John Snow made an important discovery that linked outbreaks of the killer disease cholera to polluted water pumps. Once the connection was made between clean water and better health, deaths from disease started to fall.

Changes in farming had an effect

As the population grew, there were more mouths to feed. Farmers knew they could make more money as there were increasing numbers of people needing food, so they changed the way food was produced. They used more efficient methods: selective breeding produced better quality animals, boggy land was drained, more crops were produced and new machines were invented to make farming more productive. It all took a lot of effort and money but farmers now had a financial incentive to make changes to the way food was produced. All these changes in farming have been called the **Agricultural Revolution**.

The result of the Agricultural Revolution was that more people had more meat and cereal included in their everyday meals. More food meant less hunger and better health. Better quality food meant people became stronger and were more able to fight off illnesses.

Better living conditions had an effect

In the second half of the nineteenth century, living and working conditions improved. Fresh, clean water was brought into people's houses through new pipes, and drains were installed to take waste water and sewage away from living areas. This is called better sanitation.

Housing improved and overcrowding slowly became less of a problem. Cheaper soap and the availability of water in people's houses meant that people could wash more easily and more often! Between 1760 and 1900, improvements in **public health** and sanitation reduced the risk of dying from infectious diseases.

Migration had a big effect on population

The population of the UK did not increase everywhere at the same rate. Some areas increased because of **migration**. This means people moved to certain areas either to find work and a better life or to escape hunger and poverty. Usually those **push reasons** and **pull reasons** for moving were interconnected.

Industrial towns grew fast because they attracted people looking for work or a more exciting life. The population of farming areas declined because people moved away, because there were fewer jobs as machines replaced workers.

The biggest migration was from Ireland. The population of Ireland fell as the population of Britain increased. When the Irish potato crop failed in the 1840s, millions starved. Many Irish people emigrated to the USA or chose to move to Britain, looking for a better life. Almost 1000 Irish people arrived in Glasgow each week in 1848, while thousands of others moved to areas around Liverpool before moving across Scotland and England looking for work.

The Highland Clearances were another reason why thousands of people moved within Britain and also migrated to other countries. In many cases, local farmers, called crofters, were forced off their land to make way for sheep and, later on, deer. These new sources of income for landowners required fewer employees. The crofters often had no choice but to move, and although many Highlanders emigrated to Canada or New Zealand, others ended up in the factory towns of Scotland. The old graveyard on the slopes above the New Lanark cotton **mills** has many gravestones of people who had been born in Caithness in the far north of Scotland.

> ### GLOSSARY
>
> **Public health** keeping public areas clean and healthy so that disease does not spread among the population
>
> **Migration** the movement of people, either abroad, which is emigration, or to another place within the same country
>
> **Push reason** a reason that forces people to move, such as hunger or unemployment
>
> **Pull reason** something that makes people want to move and attracts them to a different place
>
> **Mills** usually factories for making textiles such as cotton cloth

What is population distribution?

When thinking about population changes it is important to remember about **population distribution**.

Imagine students in a classroom. They would probably be spread out across the classroom evenly. This is an even distribution of people.

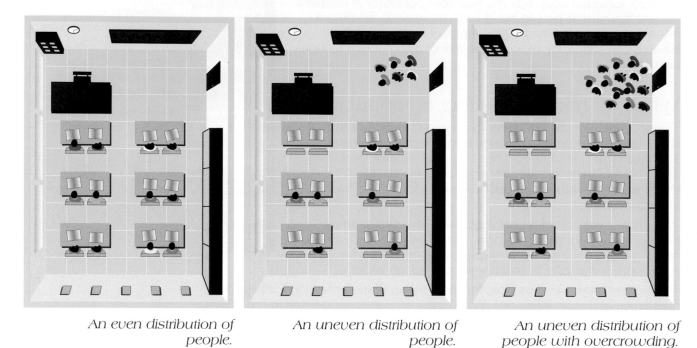

An even distribution of people.

An uneven distribution of people.

An uneven distribution of people with overcrowding.

If most students move into one corner of the classroom, the distribution of people in the room has changed but the population of the room has not changed! While part of the room is now crowded, other parts of the room are empty.

If more students then came into the room, and most also go into the same corner, then it would be very overcrowded. Meanwhile the population density of the rest of the classroom would only change slowly.

That's what happened in Britain. Some areas grew very fast, such as industrial cities that attracted workers hoping for good wages. Other areas lost population, such as Ireland or the Scottish Highlands, where people found their hard lives just getting harder. Thousands either chose to move or were forced to move.

The population distribution of the country changed. Overall, the population of Britain increased, but some areas grew very fast while some areas became **depopulated**.

To meet the needs of a growing population Britain had to change into a modern industrial country. That is what the rest of this book is about. Many of the things touched on in this chapter such as bad health, housing and working conditions are more fully explained in this book – with a focus on how things got better!

> ## GLOSSARY
>
> **Population distribution** how the population is spread across the country. Sometimes some areas grow as other areas become emptier
>
> **Depopulated** becoming emptier as people move away from an area

Activity 2

Stand up and be counted

▶ Find out when the next census will be taken.
▶ How old will you be then? Then think about the next census ten years after that.
▶ How might the information you fill in on the census form be different from the information about you already included in the last census?
▶ Some people think that running the next census will be too expensive. Can you think of an alternative method of counting people in the country or should we not bother with a census?

Activity 3

Summarise this chapter

Your task is to draw a spider diagram to summarise the reasons why the population of Britain increased after 1750.

Do some research and find out what a spider diagram is. One way is to search Google Images for 'spider diagram'. If you have access to an app called Inspiration Maps you could use that. Design an appropriate layout with the title of what you are summarising in the centre. Decide on the reasons for population growth – these should be no more than four words each. Then write these in boxes at the outside end of each leg of your diagram.

Activity 4

Quiz time

This is an individual and group activity.

Your teacher will give you three Post-its: one red, one orange and one green. You should make up three questions about the changing population of Britain between 1760 and 1900. Green should be easy (1 point), orange should be more difficult (2 points) and red the most difficult (3 points). Questions should be put on the front and answers on the back of the Post-it.

Put your initials in the bottom corner of each Post-it so everyone knows who made up the question. When you are finished, put your Post-its up on the board.

Your teacher will divide you into teams. Each member of the team should take it in turn to answer questions. Everyone should try to answer at least one question. No one should answer their own questions. Each team must try to answer at least one red, one orange and one green question.

Each correct answer scores the appropriate number of points. Incorrect answers award the appropriate points to the person who made up the question.

The team with the most points wins.

Activity 5

If this is the answer what is the question?

Below you will find a list of words or names. You have to make up a question that can only be answered by the word on the list. For example, if the word 'migration' was the answer, a question could be 'What M word means people moving?'

Here is your list of answers:

- industrialisation
- census
- depopulation

- population distribution
- Agricultural Revolution.

Question practice

National 4

Source A is from a report by a church minister writing about his parish.

SOURCE A

My parish is now in what is called an industrial area. A new factory has been built to make cotton. Homes are being put up nearby to house the numbers of new workers, more of whom seem to arrive every day. The young newlyweds produce more babies than ever before. I wonder what is going to happen to our once quiet little church.

Describe in your own words why the population of the parish is increasing. You should use Source A and your own knowledge.

Success criteria

Make at least two factual points of information, or one developed piece of information, about why the population of Britain was increasing.

National 5

Explain why the population of Britain grew so quickly in the nineteenth century. (6 marks)

In an 'explain' question you need to make six separate points from recall to gain all the marks. You will need to develop and explain your points with examples. There will not be a source in the exam to help you, but to get you started on your answer here are some hints:

You could write about:

- The effects of industrialisation.
- Better living conditions and diet.
- Changes in medical knowledge.
- Migration and population distribution.

Chapter 3 Housing

What is this chapter about?

The Industrial Revolution caused thousands of people to move into towns looking for work. Towns grew very quickly but as the population increased so did the problems of overcrowding in slums. The difficulties of poor-quality housing, overcrowding, pollution and a lack of any town planning at first led to the rapid spread of diseases. Later in the nineteenth century, housing improved. Proper sewers, fresh water and slum clearance helped to improve living conditions. Meanwhile, those who were better off bought large, new houses with gardens on the edge of towns in the suburbs.

By the end of this chapter you should be able to:

▶ Explain why living conditions were so bad in towns and cities between 1760 and 1900.
▶ Describe some of the changes that led to improvements in living conditions between 1760 and 1900.

Why did people move to the towns?

In the 1750s, most people lived in rural areas and worked on farms. However, by 1900 that had changed and the majority of the population now lived in towns and cities. The main reason to explain why towns grew so fast is that people wanted to live there. Towns provided:

▶ work
▶ entertainment
▶ excitement and the chance to make a new life and find a boyfriend or girlfriend.

The town is great! There are buses and shops and all sorts of sights. The country was boring.

I'm John McDonald and have worked on farms like my dad before me. But there's no work for me in the country now, so I thought I'd come to the town to look for work. I've got my growing family to feed.

Now we're in the town perhaps I can get a job too. It'll bring in a few shillings to help feed the kids.

I want to go back. In the country I liked to feed the animals and ride the horses. I used to help Dad on the farm.

A chatty Victorian family.

Towns grew because they had industries that needed workers. As the number of factories grew, people from the countryside began to move into the towns looking for better-paid work. Sometimes, the work was in factories making cotton cloth in large mills or sometimes the towns were smaller and specialised in making iron and steel. Other towns were near coal mines, while other towns near the coast expanded as more and more trade flowed through their ports. Bristol became a major city because of the sugar trade and Glasgow grew partly because of the trade in tobacco. However, the main point about the growth of towns is that they attracted people to live there and the number one attraction was work.

Which image is of 1750 and which is of 1900? The answer is fairly obvious but how many reasons can you give to support your answer?

Both of these pictures show Manchester.

Towns were not new: large cities such as London and Edinburgh had existed for hundreds of years. Towns that were to grow to become huge industrial centres, such as Manchester and Glasgow, were hardly more than large villages in 1750.

Glasgow in 1755 had a population of almost 24,000. By 1855, that had increased to almost 400,000. Similarly, Liverpool had grown from a town of 35,000 in 1755 to 493,000 by 1855. Manchester had increased from 45,000 to 351,000 in the same time period. Birkenhead, a village near Liverpool, had 100 people in 1801. By 1901 it had 100,000 people!

Activity 1

Factors of growth

Work out how many times Glasgow, Liverpool and Manchester had grown between 1755 and 1855 and by how much. For example, if a village of 500 people in 1755 had grown into a town of 5000 people in 1855 it would have grown by ten times ($10 \times 500 = 5000$) and it would have increased in size by 4500 people ($5000 - 500$).

In 1800, only 17 per cent of Scots lived in towns of more than 10,000 people. By 1850 that had increased to 32 per cent. By 1900, the number of Scots living in towns had grown to 50 per cent of the population.

Activity 2

Numeracy counts

Draw three pie charts (one each for the years 1800, 1850 and 1900) showing the balance between Scots in towns and Scots living in the countryside. Use the same colour code key for each pie chart.

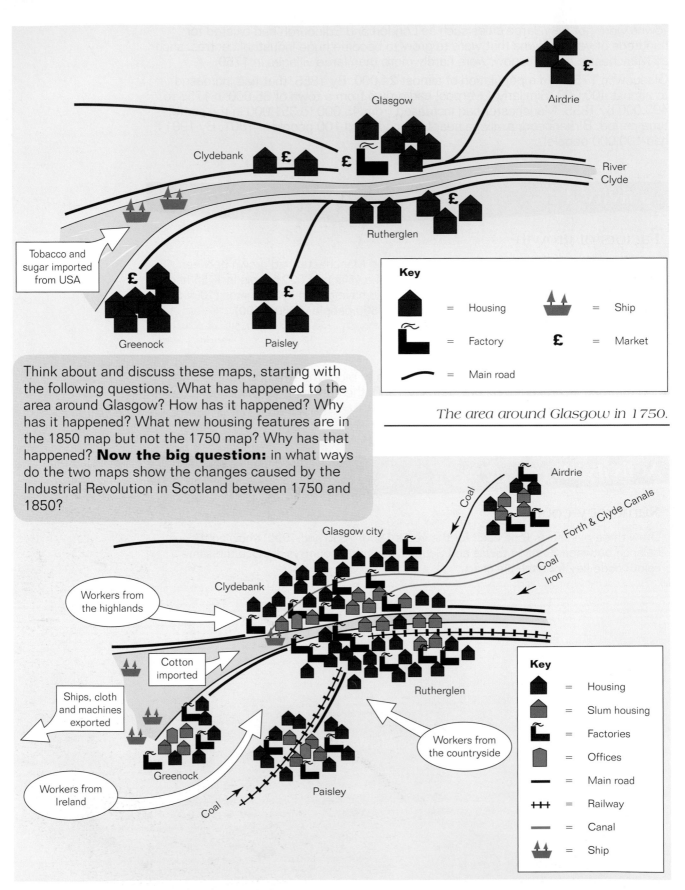

Key

🏠	=	Housing	⛵	=	Ship
⌐	=	Factory	£	=	Market
—	=	Main road			

The area around Glasgow in 1750.

Tobacco and sugar imported from USA

Think about and discuss these maps, starting with the following questions. What has happened to the area around Glasgow? How has it happened? Why has it happened? What new housing features are in the 1850 map but not the 1750 map? Why has that happened? **Now the big question:** in what ways do the two maps show the changes caused by the Industrial Revolution in Scotland between 1750 and 1850?

Workers from the highlands

Cotton imported

Ships, cloth and machines exported

Workers from Ireland

Workers from the countryside

Key

🏠	=	Housing
🏠	=	Slum housing
⌐	=	Factories
⬠	=	Offices
—	=	Main road
+++	=	Railway
—	=	Canal
⛵	=	Ship

The area around Glasgow in 1850.

What were slums like?

Bad housing, often called **slums**, had existed in British towns and cities for hundreds and hundreds of years. What made the problem of slum housing worse after 1760 was the large number of people crowding into the towns and cities. There were simply not enough houses to meet this demand. Landlords would often build poor-quality homes as fast as they could to make money from people desperate to find somewhere to stay. Some landlords also divided rooms into smaller rooms to rent to whole families.

Basic needs such as clean water and effective sewers to take away human waste were not provided. The houses had no indoor toilets and sanitation was very poor. Walls were often thin and poorly insulated from the cold and damp. Floors were either packed, hard earth or rough, wooden floorboards. There was no running water in the houses. Water was usually collected from a nearby pump or well, and the water was easily contaminated by sewage.

For most people it was important to be close to their place of work as there was no public transport. This meant that factories and housing were often close to each other. These factories produced immense amounts of pollution, making conditions in the nearby houses even more unhealthy.

Some people had to live in overcrowded **lodging houses**. There was little or no furniture and people were expected to sleep on straw or rags.

What follows is a description of the poverty in London lodging houses by the novelist Henry Fielding:

When the two little houses were emptied we found nearly 70 men and women living there. Such was the poverty of these wretches that a single loaf supplied a whole family with their food for a week.

Living conditions like these were perfect breeding grounds for diseases.

> **GLOSSARY**
>
> **Slums** very poor-quality housing, overcrowded and lacking fresh water or toilets
>
> **Lodging houses** rooms occupied by many people who paid a small rent. Usually worse than slums

> Try to list all the things the family will have to do in this one room as part of everyday life. How much space do you have in your house for all these things?

This drawing shows a family in the one room they occupy. They have no other space to live in.

How did housing improve?

The government understood that something needed to be done about the unhygienic conditions in British cities, but not everyone agreed on what was the best way to achieve this. Nevertheless, changes did happen. Cities changed as the wealthier people wanted to move away from the crowded city slums. Industrial cities were split between wealthy areas and the slums where the poor people lived.

The wealthy people of Edinburgh began to move away from the city centre. Edinburgh had a particularly bad reputation. The poor sanitation, filth and crowded streets, and especially the smoke from coal fires, had earned the capital the nickname 'Auld Reekie', meaning 'Old Smokey and Smelly'.

Wealthy people in Glasgow also followed the trend of moving away from the centre of town. The merchants, called 'Tobacco Lords', were becoming extremely wealthy thanks to the importing of tobacco in huge amounts from Britain's American colonies. They built massive new homes for themselves, starting with the impressive George Square, and followed by streets mostly named after the places that provided their wealth: Virginia, Havana and Jamaica.

Cities in England tended to follow similar patterns as those in Glasgow, as wealthy merchants looked for a way to expand their cities and improve their homes. In Bristol, for example, many large town houses were built for the sugar merchants and their families to live in, far away from the foul-smelling sugar refineries. However, the building of better houses for the wealthy did not help the thousands of people who still lived in slums. Wealthy people were happy just to get away from slum areas, not to improve them. In every city, many poor areas of slum housing still existed and they remained a hazard to public health.

The government was concerned at the spread of diseases and knew that something had to be done about living conditions. The problem could not be tackled until new laws were passed that allowed councils to buy up slum properties and then demolish them. In Scotland, the Nuisance Removal Act of 1855 gave the police the powers to clean or close properties that were a threat to the health of the public. The old problem remained, however: if slums were knocked down, where would the people who lived there move to?

1. A standpipe that supplied water to all the houses. The water came from a well next to the cesspit.
2. A communal toilet. The waste would be collected in a cesspit.
3. Filth was swept along the road.
4. The cesspit was emptied by bucket and taken away at night.
5. Back-to-back houses to fit as many people as possible in a small area.
6. People even lived in cellars.

A tenement slum yard.

A tenement room. Notice the cracked windows and that the walls are damp. There are five people living in this one room. There's no toilet and no running water. The only cooking and heating source is the fire. Where was coal kept?

Councils were given even more powers in 1875. The Public Health Act of 1875 gave town councils the ability to provide water supplies and sewers. The Artisans' and Labourers' Dwellings Improvement Act allowed councils to demolish old slum houses. Unfortunately, no more money was provided to build new, better housing. Glasgow City Council, for example, cleared hundreds of slum houses between 1875 and 1885 with the result that an estimated 30,000 people were made homeless.

One answer to homelessness was council-owned houses. Local authorities bought land, built houses and charged fair rents to tenants. After about 1900, this idea spread throughout Britain and council housing estates grew up around cities.

In most British cities in 1900 there were still problems of slums and overcrowding, but things had changed for the better. Most houses now had water supplies, toilets (often shared), sewers and gas lighting.

'Where will we live now?'

The shape of cities was also changing as the wealthier middle classes moved to the suburbs. The middle classes, who were the businessmen, bankers and office managers, and filled the many other well-paid jobs, wanted to move away from the areas where the lower classes lived. To meet that demand, larger and more impressive houses were built on the edges of towns and cities. Areas such as Morningside and Murrayfield in Edinburgh, Hillhead in Glasgow and Broughty Ferry outside Dundee became the new suburbs.

Perhaps this advertisement for the suburbs in London from *Chambers Journal* in 1844 sums up the reasons why the suburbs grew:

*Here you will find no **pestilent** gas, no belching tall industrial chimneys, nor any reeking dunghill and stagnant pools to taint the breeze and offend the nostril of passers by. The houses in the suburbs each possess a small garden.*

A photograph of a Victorian-era villa.

What about the housing for the poor?

While wealthy people tried to escape from the overcrowding, dirt and disease of the polluted cities, local town councils were also trying to improve living conditions for poor people. Slums were slowly being cleared away and new housing was built for the factory workers of the industrial towns.

Was there still a lot to do to improve housing after 1900?

In Scottish cities, row after row of tenements were built, but at least families had a front door to call their own. By now houses had to be connected to sewers and more homes were built with their own water supply, rather than having to share a water pump.

Most families used toilets that were shared. It was not until after 1900 that it became common to have a toilet for the use of only one family. Kitchens did see an improvement, however, as open fires for cooking were becoming outdated. By 1900, gas lighting and even electricity were starting to appear in some homes. Kitchen 'ranges' (coal-burning kitchen stoves) were common in most homes and provided both hot water and hot meals for the family.

Great improvements had been made to the quality of life in many of Britain's towns and cities. Wealthy people lived in large villas in the suburbs, the lower-middle class lived in new streets of terraced houses and even the new tenements were well built and airy. Many are still lived in today.

However, not everywhere had dealt with the problem of clean water and adequate sewage, and it would not be until further into the twentieth century that more improvements to the way in which people lived in towns and cities would be made. Slums still existed and this problem would not be tackled on a large scale until after the Second World War, when the remaining inner-city slum areas were cleared and people were moved to newly built, large council housing estates.

These tenements in Glasgow were built in the nineteenth century.

How can you tell these were better quality houses, built as part of housing improvements? In what ways will the interiors have changed since Victorian times? Think about sanitation, cleanliness and fuel supplies.

Activity 3

Summarise this chapter

The following summary reminds you of what this chapter has been about. Words that are important have been made into ANAGRAMS. Your task is to sort out the anagrams and then write the correct version of this summary into your workbook or work file.

The **TRIALINDUS** revolution caused thousands of people to move into **NSTOW** looking for work. As towns grew in size, the population increased but so did the problems of **DINGOCROWVER** in **MULSS**. The difficulties of poor-quality housing, overcrowding, **UTLIONPOL** and a lack of any town planning at first led to the rapid spread of diseases. Not all housing was bad. Later in the nineteenth century, **LUMS ANCECLEAR** helped to remove the worst housing. Wealthier people moved to the edges of the towns, called **URBSSUB**, where they lived in houses called **ASVILL** with **GDENSAR**.

Activity 4

The challenge! How far can you go?

The following questions go up in level of difficulty in pairs. The first two are easy. The last two are hard. How many will you try to do?

1 What is a slum?
2 What is a villa?
3 Why did industrialisation cause the growth of many towns and cities?
4 Using what you now know, how would you explain why bad housing was likely to lead to bad health?
5 Just by looking at the pictures in this chapter, what conclusions can you reach about changes in housing between 1760 and 1900?
6 Do some research by yourself to find out more than is in this chapter – but keep it relevant to the years that this course covers! Research and design a timeline showing the growth of a town or city of your choice between the mid-eighteenth century and the early twentieth century. Your timeline should include maps, pictures and some explanatory text.

Activity 5

Teach a lesson

In groups of three or four, your target is to teach a short lesson to the rest of your class which is linked to the theme of changing cities and towns between 1760 and 1900.

You must deal with the following core points:

▶ What is the link between city growth and industrialisation?
▶ What were slums and why were they so bad?
▶ How did towns and cities improve?

As in any lesson, there are really important things for you, as the teacher, to decide on and aim for:

▶ What do you want your students to be able to do and know at the end of your lesson?
▶ How will you assess the success of your lesson – in other words, what will you expect to see or hear your students doing to prove your lesson has been successful?

Your lesson should be presented in an organised, interesting, mature and informative way. Your main resource for information is this textbook but you must also research, find, beg or borrow other resources to make your lesson come alive. Think of the times you have been bored just listening to someone talk. Your lesson must be different!

Planning is vital, and everyone in your group must participate. It would be helpful to assign tasks such as a gopher to go get, a timekeeper to watch how your time is being used, a facilitator to keep things running smoothly in your group (tact and diplomacy needed here!) and a recorder to note ideas and what was suggested before you all forget.

Negotiate the length of your lesson with your teacher. About five minutes would be appropriate. It must have visual material; PowerPoint is just one of the possibilities.

Question practice

National 4

Source A is from a history textbook.

SOURCE A

As people flooded into towns and cities looking for work, builders put up houses as fast as possible. Landlords did not bother about the quality of their housing. They wanted houses built as fast as possible so they could start charging rent.

Explain in your own words why housing in industrial cities was so bad in the nineteenth century. You should use Source A and your own knowledge.

Success criteria

In your answer you should make at least two points of information about why housing in industrial cities was so bad in the nineteenth century.

National 5

Source A is from a description of housing in Glasgow written by a doctor working in the city in 1840.

SOURCE A

The working people have no thought for cleanliness. The closes and alleys are covered in the most indescribable filth due to the careless disposal of household waste. No attempt is made to clean or maintain the living quarters and waste materials are allowed to accumulate for days, or even weeks, before the inhabitants remove them. The people seem to have neither the time nor the knowledge nor the money to do anything to make their lives more bearable.

Evaluate the usefulness of Source A as evidence about the causes of poor housing conditions in British cities during the nineteenth century. You may want to comment on who wrote it, when they wrote it, why they wrote it, what they say or what has been missed out. (6 marks)

Success criteria

- To get 1 mark, you need to explain the importance of each of the points you make about the source.
- Up to 4 marks may be given for evaluative comments about origin and purpose. Comments about the origin may include an explanation about the type of source, the author or the timing of the source. Comments about purpose may include an explanation about why the source was written.
- Up to 2 marks may be given for your evaluation of the content of the source which you consider is useful in terms of the proposed question. For full marks to be given, each point needs to be discretely mentioned and its usefulness explained.
- If you list information, it will be considered to be one point and will get only 1 mark.
- Up to 2 marks may be given for evaluative comments relating to points of information not mentioned in the source.

Chapter 4 Health

What is this chapter about?

Most of the towns in Britain were dirty and unhealthy. Living conditions in the slums were a breeding ground for disease. Even by the middle of the nineteenth century there was no clear understanding of the link between bad water, overcrowding and poor health. Doctors began to suspect that dirty drinking water was a major cause of disease but improving public health cost money. Sewers, reservoirs, water pipes and drains all had to be built to supply clean water and take waste away. By 1900, public health had improved greatly, partly because of medical advances but also because of government laws that enforced improvements in sanitation.

By the end of this chapter you should be able to:

▶ Explain why bad housing had a direct connection to poor health.
▶ Describe how public health improved during the nineteenth century.

Why were people so unhealthy?

Although the population of Britain increased between 1760 and 1900, the **death rate** stayed high. The main reason for the population increasing was that more babies were being born than there were people dying.

In the growing towns and cities, early death was often caused by a lethal combination of poor diet, a dangerous working environment and bad living conditions. Small illnesses could kill people who were badly fed and weak from long hours of work. Even if people could have afforded to go to a doctor, it would not have been of much use as medical knowledge was very limited and doctors could offer no cures.

Diseases spread quickly in the overcrowded cities. Water pumps in the streets were often polluted by raw **sewage** seeping into the water system. Bad sanitation was the main problem that had to be sorted out before public health was to improve.

GLOSSARY

Death rate the number of people dying as a proportion of the entire population

Sewage human faeces and waste

How bad was the sanitation in the slum areas of cities?

Most houses lacked any form of sanitation. Sanitation means the way of getting fresh, clean water into a house and getting rid of dirty water and human waste. There was no running water and no drainage for the sewage and toilets. Toilets were called 'privies' and were usually outdoors and built over a hole in the ground, called a cesspit, where the waste collected. The privy was generally in a small wooden or brick building, with a seat made out of wooden slats. This was the type of sanitation that had existed for hundreds of years.

NATIONAL CONVENIENCES

English Convenience – the Water Closet.
Scotch Convenience. – the Bucket.
French Convenience. – le Commodités.
Dutch Convenience. – the Lake.

Explain clearly how this set of pictures links directly with the issue of health in cities, especially as more and more people crowded in during the nineteenth century.

What title would you give this cartoon?

When cesspits became full they were emptied by 'night-soil men'. These men were hired to clean out cesspits during the night and take the contents to dunghills at the edges of towns. Some houses had ash privies. Ash privies were really just wooden tubs that collected the waste. Ash or peat was then sprinkled over the waste to mask the smell. When the tub was full it was collected by the night-soil men. The main point is that there was no **sewerage** system that easily took waste away from the houses.

> ### GLOSSARY
> **Sewerage** drains and pipes (sewers) to take away sewage

What problems did bad sanitation cause?

The most obvious problem with bad sanitation was the smell, but it was not the most serious one. There were never enough privies for the population of the cities. In Dundee, in the 1860s, one housing block had only six privies for 429 tenants. Worse still were the poorly sealed or full-up cesspits that could overflow into local rivers, streams and wells, contaminating the drinking water.

Roads were crowded with horse-drawn wagons, carriages and cabs, and horse manure in the streets was another hazard for the inhabitants. The problem of crossing the street was so bad that in Edinburgh, smart ladies with long dresses had invented platform shoes called pattens. They were like little stilts or platform shoes that ladies would stand on top of so they could cross streets without dragging their dresses through the muck.

Air pollution was also a major problem in cities. Factories, furnaces and chemical plants spewed out soot and smoke into the air. City streets were often polluted with a thick smog and foul-smelling mists. Waste products were dumped into rivers, polluting them and killing all the fish. The dirty and filthy conditions, combined with poor **hygiene**, led to all sorts of ill health among the people.

GLOSSARY
Hygiene keeping things clean

'Monster Soup.' A cartoon from about 1828.

> Describe exactly what you see in this cartoon. Aim for at least six things. The beasts in the water count as one! Explain the point being made by the cartoonist.

What medical problems occurred because of poor living conditions?

When disease broke out it spread very quickly because of the overcrowded conditions. Doctors did not understand how disease was spread, as they did not yet know about germs. People had started to realise that dirty conditions were linked to disease, but they did not know exactly how people caught diseases.

This is an eyewitness account by Dr Robert Graham, from Glasgow, in 1818:

If any man wonders at the prevalence [large amount] of disease among the lower classes in Glasgow, then let him take a walk like I did this morning. Let him pick his steps among every species of disgusting filth through an alley from four to five feet wide [1.2–1.5 metres], flanked by houses five floors high. We found one lodging house fifteen feet [4.5 metres] long by nine feet [2.7 metres]. Here fifteen people slept.

> Measure out a floor area in your classroom of 4.5 m by 3 m. Now get 15 people to lie down as if they were sleeping in that space. Comment on what you think it was like to live like this.

What diseases were common in towns and cities between 1760 and 1900?

Death from disease was common and especially so for babies. Many mothers never survived childbirth. Here are the most common killer diseases:

▸ Typhus was a deadly disease spread by lice that lived on people's clothes and bedding. Everyone was covered in lice bites. The bite caused people to develop a fever, typhus fever, and it was contagious. Typhus epidemics were all too common.

▸ Influenza (the flu) was very common, and epidemics were frequent during the nineteenth century.

▸ Scarlet fever caused fear among families. It tended to affect mainly the old and very young. Many families lost all their children to the disease.

▸ Tuberculosis (TB) was spread by coughing and sneezing. People who caught it simply wasted away.

▸ Smallpox was deadly. The great smallpox outbreak in 1840 was responsible for the deaths of 12,000 people in the UK. Smallpox is highly contagious and can be transmitted by direct physical contact. In the overcrowded slums, it was easy for smallpox to spread. The smallpox virus could also survive on clothes and sheets for a week after someone had caught the disease, and because most poor people didn't have many changes of bedding or clothing, the virus was always present.

Why did problems get worse after 1831?

It soon became very clear to the government that the way that towns and cities had grown was very unhealthy and led to the spread of disease.

Neither local nor national government was handling public health very well. It was obvious that something had to be done, especially when news of a great cholera outbreak in Europe reached Britain in 1831. Between 1831 and 1832, cholera killed more than 31,000 people in the UK.

What was cholera?

Cholera was first known in what is present-day Bangladesh. No one knows why but, in around 1800, the cholera bacterium mutated (changed its form), with the result that it could now survive in the European climate. There were four great cholera outbreaks in Britain, each arriving in trade ships from the Far East and Asia.

Cholera victims had severe vomiting and diarrhoea and frequently died from dehydration. Naturally, the victim wanted to drink, but **contaminated water** was the problem. It was polluted and that was how cholera was caught in the first place. Almost 60 per cent of people who had the disease died. Cholera and other killer diseases such as typhus, smallpox and dysentery were all closely linked to bad water, overcrowding and poor diet, but doctors did not know what to do about them.

> **GLOSSARY**
> **Contaminated water** water that is polluted by poisons or dirt

How effective were early attempts to cure diseases?

Early attempts to cure diseases were not very effective, mainly because there was no real understanding of how diseases were spread. Those who believed that nasty smells were the cause argued that clearing sewage off the streets would cure everyone. Actually this was a good idea and did help to clean up towns, but many of the drains that were built to take the sewage away drained directly into the local streams and rivers – the same rivers that drinking water was taken from.

Download a version of this cartoon and label it by drawing arrows to the features and writing what you think the cartoon shows. Use these labels:
a) dead bodies being carried in coffins; b) overcrowded lodging houses;
c) an old woman searching through the midden pile for scraps to eat;
d) children playing with a dead rat; e) a child doing a headstand on the midden heap. Find out what a midden heap was made up of – remember there were no sewers! Now think: is there a connection between the reason why the cartoonist drew this picture and the reason it is included in this book?

This is a famous cartoon called 'A Court for King Cholera' drawn in 1852. In this sense the word 'court' has two meanings. The cartoon shows a courtyard and it suggests that the disease of cholera will spread easily there. The other, older meaning is a place where a king rules over his subjects and is totally in charge. In this sense cholera is the king. Look closely at this cartoon or use Google Images to find a larger version.

A cartoon drawn in 1866.

What point do you think the cartoonist was trying to make about the spread of disease in cities? Look at this drawing and the cartoon above. Do you think the two drawings fully show the cause of disease in mid-nineteenth-century cities?

The problem of water

Doctors began to suspect that dirty drinking water was a major cause of disease. In London, a doctor called John Snow made the link between drinking water polluted by human waste and outbreaks of cholera. Most people collected their water from pumps in the street. One pump provided the water supply for hundreds of people. People had to carry their water from the pump to their homes in buckets, so naturally they used the pump closest to their houses.

By mapping the water wells in an area where every cholera victim lived, Dr Snow found that most cholera victims were concentrated around one water well pump: the Broad Street pump.

What did parliament do to improve matters?

The 1831 Board of Health

When cholera first arrived in Britain, it spread fast, reaching both London and Edinburgh by 1832.

The government set up a Board of Health to look for ways to solve the problem. This was the first time that national government got directly involved in organising local authorities to deal with problems. It was also the first time that the importance of good hygiene was emphasised by the government. The Board of Health suggested that anyone with cholera should be quarantined (kept way from other people) and infected bedding and clothes be destroyed to prevent the spread of infection. But did they really know what they were doing?

People taking water from wells other than the one in Broad Street did not suffer so much from cholera. Discoveries like this helped to persuade local authorities that they needed to spend money on providing fresh water for all the people and that sewers, reservoirs and drains had to be built.

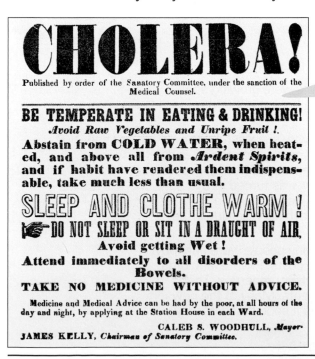

If cholera broke out in your area and you read this poster, how worried would you be and why?

A poster warning of cholera and offering advice.

How successful were the Boards of Health?

Fear of the cholera outbreak was so big that many towns and cities accepted the suggestions and set up their own Boards of Health, with health inspectors. However, the local Boards of Health had no powers to make people clean up their properties or even force people to stay quarantined. When the first cholera epidemic started to fade, local Boards of Health broke up with arguments between members about the cost of taking action and what the best ways of stopping another cholera outbreak were.

Who was Edwin Chadwick?

One of the early pioneers in public health was Edwin Chadwick. Chadwick ordered an investigation into why diseases broke out and what could be done to stop such epidemics. His report, called the *Sanitary Conditions of the Labouring Population of Great Britain*, was published in 1842, and shocked those who wanted to believe that poor people were responsible for their own problems.

Chadwick's report stated clearly that:

▶ Disease was not the fault of the poor working class. Instead, he said it was caused by filth and dirt on the streets.
▶ Overcrowding was a main reason why disease spread quickly.
▶ The lack of clean drinking water was a likely cause of much disease.

Chadwick's report was directly responsible for a new government law: the Public Health Act of 1848.

What did the Public Health Act of 1848 do?

The first thing the Public Health Act did was to set up a new Board of Health, with Chadwick in charge. Chadwick then ordered towns to set up their own Boards of Health. These new local health boards would have the power to enforce new laws such as:

▶ All new homes must have proper drains and lavatories.
▶ House owners must link their drains to the main sewers.
▶ Landlords must provide clean water for their tenants.
▶ Rubbish bin collections were organised, paid for by a local tax.

How successful was the Public Health Act of 1848?

Before 1800, very few sewers had actually been built. Towns were growing so fast that nobody had worked out a way to deal with all the extra human waste produced every day.

At first it looked as if the 1848 Public Health Act would be very successful. Many cities reduced their death rates almost by half by 1858 and many other towns and cities built new sewers, improved their water supplies and employed health inspectors to enforce the new regulations. Loch Katrine, near Glasgow, was turned into a reservoir and was able to provide 200 million litres of clean water every day to the city. Edinburgh Council piped fresh water from St Mary's Loch near Selkirk in the Scottish Borders.

However, there was a lot of criticism about the new act. Many people were unhappy about paying the local taxes that were needed to cover the costs. Private landlords resented the local authorities telling them what to do with their properties. The wealthier people in towns objected to paying for improvements. Many of the new sewers drained the waste into local rivers and streams, and it soon found its way back into the drinking water.

This drawing shows sewers being built. Think of what that means – every house linked to a sewer, every street with a network of sewers underneath. Why was it so difficult to provide good sanitation to houses in growing cities? If you were a town planner, what would be your biggest problems in providing improved sanitation?

Chadwick became a very unpopular man. When his improvements failed to prevent another outbreak of cholera in 1853, people said that his ideas were all wrong. He was eventually sacked in 1854 and his Board of Health was closed in 1858.

How was public health improved throughout the nineteenth century?

From the late 1850s onwards, parliament passed a series of laws aimed at improving public health.

The Sanitary Act of 1866 gave town councils the power to force landowners and builders to connect new houses to sewers even if the owners did not want to do it. Local authorities were also given the power to order the landlords of a slum property to improve conditions, and if they did not, then the authorities could order demolition on the grounds of the houses being dangerous to public health.

The 1875 Public Health Act applied to every part of Britain, not just the industrial cities. Before 1875 the government had issued 30 new laws all dealing with public health. The problem was that so many laws just added to confusion and they were difficult to enforce. What the 1875 Public Health Act did was to bring together the main points of all the previous laws. Now that there was only one Public Health Act, it was easier for local authorities to enforce.

Every community, town and parish had to have a public Board of Health, responsible for looking after its community. Every Board of Health had to have at least one inspector and local authorities were given new powers to pave roads and light streets, to build new reservoirs to provide clean water, to provide public toilets and also to set up parks for recreation.

Meanwhile in Scotland, the Public Health (Scotland) Act of 1867 allowed local authorities to appoint medical officers of health and to charge a general rate (local tax) on householders for public health purposes. However, only a few local authorities appointed full-time medical officers of health. It was not until the Local Government (Scotland) Act of 1889 that county councils had to appoint medical officers of health in order to control and check the provision of improvements in the health of the country.

In the later nineteenth century, there was also a large hospital building programme in Scotland. For example, the Dundee Women's Hospital developed from a dispensary for women and children, set up in the 1890s for the treatment of women by female doctors. The Dundee Eye Institution was established in 1836 to provide a free service to those who could not afford treatment for their eyes. In 1879, the Edinburgh Royal Infirmary moved to a huge new building, then on the edge of the town near the Meadows. The Royal Infirmary represented the latest advances in medical treatment when it opened its new building in 1879. Meanwhile the Glasgow Royal Infirmary, originally opened in 1794, was expanded with a specialist fever block in 1829 and a surgical block in 1861.

What improvements were there in medical knowledge at this time?

In 1865 a French chemist, named Louis Pasteur, was able to prove that germs caused disease and not the other way round.

Until that time, people knew that germs existed, but could not agree on how they formed. Pasteur was now able to look for vaccinations by targeting the germs first.

Pasteur died before he could find the vaccine for cholera, but a German scientist, Robert Koch, carried on his work. Koch was able to discover the causes of deadly diseases such as anthrax and tuberculosis and in 1883, while in India, he discovered (like John Snow) that cholera was caught from drinking contaminated water.

As doctors and scientists became more familiar with germs and how they were spread, this helped town planners and local authorities to understand how to prevent outbreaks of deadly diseases.

Was public health better in 1900 than it had been in 1760?

By 1900, public health had improved greatly compared to 1760. The improvements were mainly due to better housing, clean water and sanitation, better diet, improved living standards and advances in medical knowledge. Towns and cities now had efficient drains and sewers to take waste away and gradually flush toilets began to appear in people's houses or in public lavatories.

Despite the improvements since 1760, slums and poverty still existed in 1900. Poor people could not escape to villas in the suburbs and find the money to have flush toilets installed. In 1900, a study of the living conditions of poor people in York reported:

Smell of room from dirt and bad air unbearable. Dirty bedding strewn over floor. Nearby 16 families are sharing one water tap. The grating under the water tap is used for the disposal of human excreta [poo!] and was partly blocked with it when inspected.

Health and housing had improved, but not for everyone.

Make up your own advertising jingle for Mr Crapper's new invention!

A magazine advertisement for a new type of toilet.

Activity 1

Summarise this chapter

The following summary reminds you of what this chapter has been about. Words that are important have been made into ANAGRAMS. Your task is to sort out the anagrams and then write the correct version of this summary into your workbook or work file.

There was a clear link between **DAB VINGLI** *conditions and* **DAB LEATHH**. *Living conditions in the* **SMULS** *were perfect breeding grounds for* **SEASEDIS** *such as* **ERACHOL** *and* **PHUSTY**. *People had little knowledge of what caused diseases and even less on how to* **ERCU** *them. By 1900 things had improved. Better* **ICALMED** *knowledge and new laws to improve* **LICPUB LTHHEA** *were important in making Britain a healthier place.*

Activity 2

If this is the answer what is the question?

Below you will find a list of words or names. You have to make up a question that can only be answered by the word on the list. For example, if the word 'typhus' was the answer, a question could be 'Which disease was spread by lice bites?'

Here is your list of answers:

- cholera
- public health
- sewers
- Crapper
- Pasteur
- Edinburgh Royal Infirmary
- Chadwick
- Boards of Health.

Activity 3

Write a question

Your task now is to write an 'explain' question which asks how health improved in Britain between 1760 and 1900. Explain questions often start like this: 'Explain the reasons why …'. To be successful in answering this type of question you must give five or six reasons why something happened, so your question must allow someone to make that same number of points in the answer.

You will be able to check you have allowed for a wide-enough question when you write your own mark scheme for the question. That means you must list the points you would expect to see in a good answer. This question is worth 5 or 6 marks so you must include at least 5 or 6 points in your mark scheme.

When you have completed this task, exchange your work with a partner and you can answer their question while they answer yours. After ten minutes stop writing, give your work to your partner and she or he will mark your answer while you mark theirs.

Question practice

National 4

Use the historical information in this chapter and anything else you can discover to design an information poster. This information poster should show the following:

- The health problems in Britain between 1760 and 1900.
- What was done to improve public health.

There are a variety of ways you can design this. A few ideas are listed below.

- You may wish to divide your information poster into 'before' and 'after' the improvements brought about by new laws.
- Or, you could present the information in the form of a leaflet, a mindmap or a storyboard that details the improvements in health.
- There may also be an opportunity for you to design a slideshow presentation that can be shared with the class or shown on your school's website for revision.
- You could produce your own images and display them on your information poster to make a collage.

It is important to remember that you will only be assessed on your historical understanding and not on the artistic qualities of your information poster. However, it should be presented in a clear and neat manner to allow your audience to fully understand your main ideas.

National 5

This is a 'how fully' question. In this type of question you need to select the points from the source which are relevant to the question. Usually there will be three points in the source. Then, to get full marks, you need to bring in points from recall that are also relevant to the question.

Source A describes improvements that led to improved health in British cities during the nineteenth century.

SOURCE A

People living in Britain's cities at the beginning of the nineteenth century suffered terrible living conditions. There were a number of changes that brought about improvements in health during the century. These included the control and then the steady reduction of lethal diseases of childhood. This was achieved by improvement of the urban environment through the provision of cleaner water and better sewerage. The efforts of doctors, nurses and midwives were also beginning to be felt in working-class communities.

How fully does Source A describe the improvements that led to better health in Britain's cities in the nineteenth century? (6 marks)

You should make a decision about how fully the source describes improvements that match up with your own knowledge. You should then support your view by mentioning things in the source that support your point of view. You should then say that the source does not mention important points about health improvements, it does not tell us much about how, why and when these improvements were made.

Chapter 5 Cotton

What is this chapter about?

By the end of the eighteenth century, cotton cloth was being made in factories. As demand for cotton cloth increased, new inventions caused the domestic system of cloth production to be replaced by a new factory system. In the mills, steam-powered machines did the jobs of spinning and weaving. After 1760, factories and mills spread across industrial Britain attracting tens of thousands of men, women and children looking for work. Many factory workers were children. They worked long hours and sometimes started work as young as four or five years old. Inside the factory, the noise of machines was deafening and the heat was often suffocating. Fingers, hair and clothing often got trapped in the machines leading to severe injuries or death. Eventually, conditions grew so bad that some people demanded laws to improve working conditions in the mills.

By the end of this chapter you should be able to:

▶ Describe working conditions in cotton mills around 1800.
▶ Explain why working conditions were so dangerous in mills.
▶ Describe the improvements that took place in mills because of technological advances up to 1900.
▶ Describe the improvements that took place in mills because of changes in the law up to 1900.

How is cloth made?

For thousands of years people have dressed in clothes made from **textiles**. Whether the clothes are made from wool or cotton or silk or linen, the basic way of making textiles, or cloth, is always the same. The individual fibres of the cotton or linen (from the flax plant) or strands of wool or silk all have to be spun and stretched into one long continuous thread or yarn.
A ball of wool, for example, is one long continuous strand of wool. The process of making the long continuous thread is called spinning.

The threads have to be bound together to make a piece of cloth. Wool is thick enough to be woven or knitted. The other fibres are woven. To weave thread or yarn into cloth **weavers** use a device called a loom.

> **GLOSSARY**
> **Textiles** a general word for different types of cloth
> **Weavers** people who make cloth on a loom

A woman using a spinning wheel.

A man using a loom to weave cloth.

What was the domestic system?

Before 1760, most cloth was made in people's own homes using handlooms and simple spinning wheels. Making cloth was known as a cottage industry because the work was done in people's cottages. It was also called the domestic system. For centuries skilled craftsmen worked in their own homes, making things for local markets. Craftsmen could work to their own hours, working when they needed to. Many had farms that they worked on during the day and then they spent their evenings on their cottage industry.

In the domestic system of making cloth, one family might be **spinners**, making thread on their spinning wheels, before passing it along to another family of weavers who wove the thread into cloth on handlooms. The finished cloth would then be picked up by merchants who sold it at markets.

After 1760, the Industrial Revolution made big changes to the textile industry. These changes involved *where* and *how* the spinning and weaving happened.

GLOSSARY

Spinners people who spin fibres into long threads or yarn

Mechanisation using machines, instead of people making things by hand

Why did the domestic system end?

The simple answer is that the domestic system of cloth production could not supply enough cloth or produce consistently good quality. It was the demand for cotton cloth that led to the **mechanisation** of the textile industry, based in factories.

Unlike wool and linen, raw cotton could not be grown in Britain. Instead, large amounts of raw cotton – rather like cotton-wool balls – arrived in Britain from the USA. It is no accident that the new cotton-making industry grew up within reach of the ports where cotton was imported – Liverpool and Glasgow. Cotton cloth was hugely popular. It was lightweight and easy to wash and dry. Manufacturers could sell as much as they could produce and they were determined to increase production by introducing new technology.

How did mechanisation change the cotton industry?

Just like today, there were people who see a market for goods or services and think of ways to turn that opportunity into profit. These people are called **entrepreneurs** – businesspeople if you like. Often entrepreneurs work closely with inventors. After all, there is not much point wasting time inventing things if they are not much use or don't make money. Around 1760, entrepreneurs and inventors saw that if they could produce more cotton cloth quickly and cheaply to meet the growing demand then they would make a fortune!

As new machines were invented to make the production of cotton cloth faster and better, a place had to be found to use them. New machines were too big and too expensive for people's homes. It also made economic sense to put lots of the machines together in one large building and bring the workers to the machines, rather than each worker having their own machine, which is what happened in the domestic system.

The word 'manufacture' means to make something, and the big places where cotton was produced in large amounts were called manufactories – or factories for short.

As well as a building, the new machines also needed a power source. They were mostly too big to be worked by human muscle power. The first power source used was water.

Water wheels were not a new invention. They had been used for hundreds of years, for example, to power corn mills. Flowing water turned a large wheel that was connected by big belts or spindles and axles to anything the factory or mill owner wanted to turn.

It was the use of water wheels to power new machinery that helped to spark the Industrial Revolution. New inventions focused on spinning and weaving and new innovations appeared quickly. Each new machine tried to improve on the previous one by making cloth faster and in greater and greater quantities.

In 1733, John Kay invented the flying **shuttle**. On a loom, a weaver had to push a shuttle carrying thread or yarn from one side to the other. That meant the width of the cloth being made depended on how far the weaver could stretch. The flying shuttle powered the shuttle from side to side, making it possible for weavers to make bundles of cloth up to four times wider than before.

Inventor James Hargreaves had made machines for people to use in their own homes. He invented the spinning jenny which fed thread into eight wooden spindles at the same time, instead of just one, so it produced thread eight times more quickly than doing it by hand.

The inventions of Kay and Hargreaves were still used in the domestic system but then industrialisation arrived!

Four years after Hargreaves had shown people how to produce more thread, Richard Arkwright saw the possibilities of turning spinning into a factory process.

Arkwright's water frame, invented in 1769, was powered by a water wheel attached to his mill at Cromford in Derbyshire. The mill was a success and Arkwright made a fortune. Arkwright developed other water-powered mills, and eventually mills that were powered by steam engines.

What words would you use to describe the scene in this image? What words would you use to describe the production shown?

A water-powered cotton mill.

Did Arkwright create the factory age?

Although early water frames could only drive four spindles at once, Arkwright kept all his frames under one roof and had them working 24 hours a day. Workers toiled at the machines in 12-hour shifts. The yarn produced by the frame was of a much better quality than that made by the spinning jenny and output was significantly increased. The factory age had begun. Now the race was on to produce more and more cotton cloth to keep up with demand.

 Ten years later, in 1779, Samuel Crompton invented the spinning mule. It combined the best elements of the spinning jenny and the water frame and at first could operate 48 spindles at a time. By 1830, spinning mules were automatically turning 1200 spindles at a time.

In the space of one generation, the old domestic system of spinning thread was destroyed. In 1760, working in the domestic system, *one* thread could be spun in the same time that now, in 1830, 1200 threads could be spun. There was now so much thread being produced that weavers, who still worked mainly in their own homes, had plenty of work to do. After all, weavers were still needed to turn thread into cloth!

 Production changed again and this time the weavers faced the challenges of mechanisation. By the 1780s, a Scottish engineer called James Watt made improvements to a fairly new invention: the steam engine. Watt developed a new series of gears that could be attached to the engine, making it capable of turning wheels. Now that there was a reliable steam engine that could be connected to other machines, the steam age had begun, and the Industrial Revolution in textiles could really take off.

The power loom was invented by Edmund Cartwright in 1785 and could produce four times as much cloth as a handloom weaver. However, the real change was that the machine was operated by a power source – steam – rather than by hand. The machine was improved many times and eventually the looms could be used non-stop. It meant that factories could run for 24 hours a day. These new machines produced better quality cotton cloth but perhaps the biggest effect was on the people who worked in the textile industry.

In what very important way is the scene shown in this factory very different from the scene shown on page 37?

A cotton mill with a power loom.

What was it like to work in the new factories?

The need for skilled workers disappeared as machines became more automatic. In 1760, spinning and weaving to make cotton were skilled jobs. By 1900, cloth was made by machines and any unskilled worker – even a child – could be used to look after the machines. This meant that wages were lower and more and more women and children, who could be paid even less, were employed. Those workers who considered themselves skilled and demanded higher wages found themselves without jobs. Women and children could easily do the same work and be paid a lot less. Many men found themselves at home unemployed as their wives and daughters were working in factories.

Factories and mills gave employment to tens of thousands of men, women and children. They worked long hours and sometimes started work as young as four or five years old.

Why would mill owners prefer to employ a child like this?

Most cotton mills worked their employees very hard. When Richard Arkwright set up his Cromford mill, he made his employees work 12-hour shifts. While working in the domestic system, the weavers and spinners could set up their own workshops and decide when they worked and for how long. In contrast, strict discipline was used in the factory system to force workers to adjust to the new way of working.

Working conditions were harsh. Factory hooters sounded at about 5a.m. Workers had no other way of telling the time, so they hurried to the factory in fear of being late; for which they could be sacked. Without jobs, the workers would be homeless and starving.

Modern ideas of health and safety at work did not exist in the nineteenth century. As a result, many factories

A child working in the spinning room of a mill.

If this was one room in a large factory of 100 rooms, how many people would work in the whole factory? Can you think why discipline had to be strict?

An artist's impression of a factory.

were very dangerous places. Many of the new machines had moving parts that were exposed. There were a lot of accidents.

In some mills as many as two-thirds of the workers could be children. Children's work in factories was thought of as normal and even useful. There was no childcare at home, so when mothers went out to work they took their children with them. The children would be able earn a little money. Factory owners justified employing children by saying that if they did not employ them then they would be just left at home or wandering the streets.

Young children would be employed to crawl between the moving machines to sweep up cotton waste so that it could be reused. When threads broke, older children or women would retie the threads while the machines were still running. Often workers could get their hair or fingers trapped in the machinery.

Those in charge of the child workers, the 'overseers', were often brutal, beating the children for not working fast enough or for falling asleep during the long shifts.

The factories were often poorly ventilated. The air was thick with dust and fluff from the cotton. The smell of oil, grease and sweat was sickening. It was also very hot. Humidity was kept high to stop the cotton threads from breaking as the machines wove the threads into cloth. People could faint and pass out from the conditions. That was when accidents happened and people could fall into the machines. If that was not bad enough, open toilet buckets stood near the workers.

Discipline was tough. Workers were not allowed to talk or whistle or in any way distract themselves from their jobs. This went on day after day with only Sundays off. There were no holidays. In 1831, there was an inquiry into children's working hours in cotton factories. The following source comes from a question and answer section of the inquiry's report:

Q: When the mills were busy, at what time in the morning did the girls start work?
A: They have started work at about three o'clock in the morning and ended at ten at night.
Q: Have you not great difficulty in awakening your children at this time?
A: Yes, we had to lift them asleep and shake them as we dressed them.
Q: Have your children ever been strapped? [Beaten with a leather belt.]
A: Yes, every one. The eldest daughter's back was beaten nearly to a jelly.

Eventually, conditions grew so bad that some people demanded laws to improve the working environment in the mills. However, there was an exception to poor working conditions in cotton mills and that was to be found in New Lanark, near Lanark, on the banks of the River Clyde.

Activity 1

Numeracy counts

▶ On a normal school day, how many hours and minutes pass between you getting up in the morning and going to bed at night?

▶ How many hours and minutes do you spend each day working in school?

Now imagine that you are a mill worker in the 1860s:

▶ Multiply your previous answers by 6 (this was the number of working days in your week).

▶ How many hours you would spend working in the mill?

▶ The pay was 15–35p per week with a 14-hour working day, strict rules and regular beatings and fines. How would you feel about that life?

How was New Lanark different from most other mills?

In 1784, David Dale, along with Richard Arkwright, built four large mills just downriver from the Falls of Clyde near Lanark. The reason for this location was the availability of water to power Arkwright's water frame. New Lanark became the largest cotton-making factory in Scotland, employing 2500 people by the 1860s.

Most people think of factories as dirty, smelly places. Is there anything that surprises you about this picture showing the New Lanark factories? What reasons can you suggest to explain the *location* of New Lanark mills? What else can you see that would have to be built given the location of New Lanark?

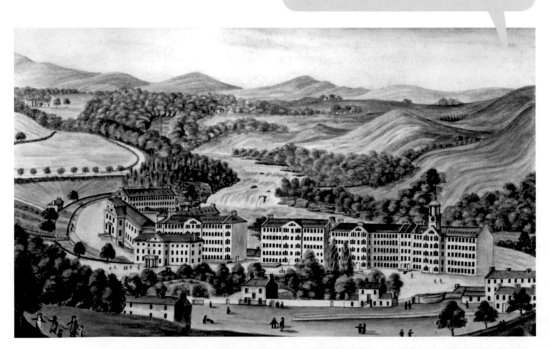

A painting of the New Lanark mills in about 1818. New Lanark is today known as a World Heritage site. People come from all over the world to visit it.

Who was Robert Owen?

Robert Owen brought important changes that are still famous worldwide. Owen married Dale's daughter and became manager of New Lanark in 1800. Owen's ideas were thought of as strange at the time. He believed that if employees were well treated, they then would respond by being good workers. Owen also believed that people should live in healthy conditions, they should receive good quality food and, most importantly, young children should be given an education rather than forced to work.

As manager of the cotton mills, Owen treated workers well and reduced the length of the working day. Other mill owners laughed and said that such changes would not enforce discipline and New Lanark would lose money. They were wrong. Production from the mills increased and so did profits. Perhaps the most famous thing Owen did was to stop the use of physical punishments. Workers could no longer be beaten. Instead, discipline was enforced by the silent monitor.

Above each worker's machine, Owen hung a cube. Four sides were painted in a different colour. Each colour represented a quality of work. White meant your work was very good. Yellow meant your work was OK. Blue meant your work should be improved but, worst of all, when the black face of the cube showed, everyone else could see your work was very bad! Imagine the embarrassment when the overseer turned your cube to black. Many people say that the phrase 'Ah felt black affronted', meaning 'I was embarrassed', comes from New Lanark!

Owen's silent monitor.

Why is Owen still important today?

Owen's ideas are really important to us even today. He started one of the first **co-operative** shops where workers could get good quality food at reasonable prices. The more they spent, the more they got back in from the profits of the shop.

Owen also made up a list of rules and regulations for the people living in the company's houses. These were to ensure that the houses and streets were kept clean and safe. He employed a committee to inspect the houses, and make sure people were following the rules. This committee became known as the 'bug hunters' but they did help to keep the village a clean and healthy place to live.

Finally, Owen became famous for his treatment of children. While other mill owners worked their children for over 12 hours a day and beat them if they spoke or whistled or fell asleep, Owen believed children should be treated well and wrote about his ideas in 1833:

Eight hours' daily labour is enough for any human being. They must have an ample supply of food, clothing and shelter, or the necessaries and comforts of life, and for the remainder of his time, every person is entitled to education, recreation and sleep.

Robert Owen felt that education was important. He built two buildings to school the adults and children of New Lanark. The Institute for the Formation of Character was the first to be built. It held evening classes, school lessons and social events.

Owen's model of looking after workers is still copied today. The fact that Owen made a profit from New Lanark gained him credibility. He proved that commercial success could be achieved without exploitation of young workers.

> **GLOSSARY**
>
> **Co-operative** a non-profit business run for the benefit of those using its services

In this image the children are at school. In what ways are Owen's ideas still seen in schools? Why is Owen still remembered as an important man today?

A painting entitled 'Mr Owen's Institution, New Lanark, 1825.'

How did the conditions for factory workers improve?

Although working conditions in textile mills were bad, improvements slowly began to happen. Robert Owen showed at New Lanark that it was possible to treat workers well and still make a profit but most factory owners were only interested in making as much money as they could. The only thing that would make working conditions improve would be new laws. These new laws, called the Factory Acts, were passed by parliament and aimed to limit the number of hours worked by women and children in the textile industry.

At first, factory owners found ways of getting around the new laws. For example, the Factory Act of 1802 reduced working hours but there were no inspectors to see that owners obeyed the new law. Many mill owners just ignored the rules and carried on as before, knowing they would not be found out and punished.

The same problem was faced with the Factory Act of 1819. The law was to stop children under the age of nine working in mills and limit the hours of work for children under 16. Once again, the law failed because there were no inspectors to make sure that factory and mill owners obeyed the law.

People who tried change things for the better were called reformers and an important early factory reformer was Lord Ashley, the Earl of Shaftesbury. He was also an MP and a very religious man. He saw it as his religious duty to help those less fortunate than himself. Lord Ashley became the leader of the factory reformers in parliament and he was responsible for getting MPs to agree to investigate just how bad the working conditions were in factories. Inspectors toured hundreds of factories and mills, gathering evidence about the working conditions of children. They reported their findings back to parliament, who were horrified at the results. In the end, parliament agreed to introduce another Factory Act.

What did the Factory Act of 1833 do?

The Factory Act of 1833 made it illegal for children under the age of nine to be employed in factories. It also said that children between the ages of nine and 13 were only allowed to work a total of nine hours a day, up to a maximum of 48 hours a week. Teenagers between 13 and 18 were also limited to working 12 hours a day and 69 hours a week. It also ruled that only people over the age of 18 could work at night. However, far more important than that, was the introduction of government inspectors. These inspectors had the right to enter any factory they pleased at any time of day and make sure the new laws were being followed. Any factory or mill owners who were breaking the law would then be prosecuted.

Was this Factory Act successful?

The 1833 Factory Act was a major step forward in improving the working conditions of children. Younger children were now protected from being exploited and older children now had a reduced workload. More importantly, government inspectors did try to ensure mill owners followed the new rules.

However, the inspectors did not have any powers themselves to force people to obey the laws. It was also difficult for the inspectors to find out if mill owners were breaking the law. Not all the children were registered at birth, so it was sometimes difficult to find out their real ages.

Perhaps the most surprising problem for this act was that the parents of the working children did not like it. They thought that it was not the job of government to interfere in their lives. Many believed that if the children were not at work then they would just get into mischief. Most families needed the money earned by their children in order to survive. Therefore, many families helped the mill owners to ignore the new laws and fool the inspectors.

What was the Ten Hours Act?

During the 1840s, reformers struggled to get laws enforcing a maximum working day of ten hours. At that time it was common for workers to spend an average of 12.5 hours per day working in tiring, dangerous conditions. When the time spent going to and from the mills was added on, the working day stretched to 14.5 hours.

> Research the name of the author of this collection of letters – Nassau Senior – and discover how he felt about the Factory Act reform campaign.

LETTERS

ON THE

FACTORY ACT,

As it affects the Cotton Manufacture,

ADDRESSED TO

THE RIGHT HONOURABLE

THE PRESIDENT OF THE BOARD OF TRADE,

BY

NASSAU W. SENIOR, ESQ.

TO WHICH ARE APPENDED,

A LETTER TO MR. SENIOR FROM LEONARD HORNER, ESQ.

AND

MINUTES OF A CONVERSATION BETWEEN

MR. EDMUND ASHWORTH, MR. THOMSON AND MR. SENIOR.

LONDON:

B. FELLOWES, LUDGATE STREET.

1837.

The title page of a collection of letters, published four years after the Factory Act of 1833.

The Factory Act of 1844 was the first law to try to make machinery safer as well as to reduce working hours further.

Women and young people now worked the same number of hours – no more than 12 hours a day during the week, including one and a half hours for meals, and nine hours on Sundays. For the first time, machinery was to be fenced in and accidental deaths were to be investigated.

Pressure from reformers continued and the Factory Act of 1847, also known as the Ten Hours Act, restricted the working hours of women and children in British factories to ten hours a day.

Other Factory Acts followed, and by 1878 children under the age of ten had to go to school and not work in mills. Children aged 10–14 could only be employed for half days and women were to work no more than 56 hours a week.

Were factories a better place to work by 1900?

Compared to 1800, the conditions in factories were considerably better in 1900. Hours were shorter and there was more protection from accidents. However, even after 1900 the working conditions were poor compared to what people expect today. Employees still worked long hours and received poor pay, the machines were still dangerous, at least compared to modern ones, and factory conditions still depended on how much the factory owner was prepared to do to help the workers.

Activity 2

Summarise this chapter

The following summary reminds you of what this chapter has been about. Words that are important have been made into ANAGRAMS. Your task is to sort out the anagrams and then write the correct version of this summary into your workbook or work file.

Before the Industrial Revolution most people dressed in clothes made from **LOOW** or **NENLI**. Clothes were made in the homes of **NNERSSPI** and **VERSWEA**. This was part of the **ESTICDOM TEMSYST**.

As demand for cotton increased, inventors created new machines to spin thread more quickly. Two of these inventions were the **NINGSPINN ENNJY** and the **TERWA MEFRA**. The new machines were too big to be used in small houses so new, large **TORIESFAC** were built, also known as cotton **LLSMI**.

Conditions in the mills were hard. Working hours were long and there was harsh discipline. **DRENCHIL** as young as **VEFI** worked in mills. Eventually new laws improved conditions and made the machines safer.

Activity 3

If this is the answer what is the question?

Below you will find a list of words or names. You have to make up a question that can only be answered by the word on the list. For example, if the word 'Cotton' was the answer, a question could be 'what C became a popular textile in the eighteenth and nineteenth centuries?'

Here is your list of answers:

▶ domestic system
▶ loom
▶ mill
▶ Owen
▶ steam power loom
▶ spinning jenny
▶ 1833
▶ Ten Hours
▶ New Lanark
▶ nine years of age.

Activity 4

Just a minute

This is a group activity and should be played between teams of three or four. You will be asked to play a game called 'Just a minute'.

Your group must research and then nominate one of you to talk about a topic related to the production of cotton cloth.

Suggested topics are listed below. You can add your own topics if you wish.

▶ Technology in mills.
▶ Why cotton mills were developed.
▶ How workers were treated in mills.
▶ How the Factory Acts helped to improve working conditions.

Planning is vital, and everyone in your group must participate. It would be helpful to assign tasks such as a researcher to get information or ideas, a timekeeper to watch how your time is being used, a facilitator to keep things running smoothly in your group (tact and diplomacy needed here!) and a recorder to note ideas before you all forget.

You must talk for a whole minute, without hesitation or repeating yourself.

If you get to the end of the minute without breaking the rules, you will get points.

Other teams can challenge you if they think you have broken the rules. If their challenge is judged to be correct, they will get a point and then can take over the remaining time. If their challenge is not correct, you will get a point and get to carry on speaking.

The team with the most points wins.

Question practice

National 4

Source A was written by a visitor to a cotton mill in Bolton, Lancashire, in 1847.

SOURCE A

The workers are well clothed and fed. The mill is a large building and kept very clean. The working rooms had many windows in each room. I saw that great care had been taken to put guards on dangerous machinery. I was told accidents were very rare and were caused by the stupidity of the workers.

How useful is Source A as evidence about working conditions in cotton mills in the nineteenth century?

Success criteria

▶ You must write an answer that makes it clear whether you think the source is useful or not.
▶ You should support your opinion by explaining in your own words: who wrote the source, when was the source written and what does the source tell us about working in the cotton mills?

National 5

This is a 'how fully' question. In this type of question you need to select the points from the source which are relevant to the question. Usually there will be three points in the source. Then, to get full marks, you need to bring in points from recall that are also relevant to the question.

Source A was written by a visitor to a cotton mill in Bolton, Lancashire, in 1847.

SOURCE A

The factory people are better clothed and fed than many other working-class people. I found the mill to be a large building and very clean. The working rooms were spacious and well ventilated. There were many windows in each room. I observed that great care had been taken to put guards on dangerous machinery. I was told accidents in the factory were very rare and were caused by stupidity or negligence by the worker. However, accidents did occur.

How fully does Source A describe working conditions in British cotton mills in the nineteenth century? (6 marks)

You should make a decision about how fully the source describes conditions that match up with your own knowledge. You should then support your view by mentioning things in the source that support your point of view. You should then say that the source does not mention important points about working conditions in mills; it does not tell us much about how, why and when these conditions changed.

Chapter 6 Coal

What is this chapter about?

Coal was the fuel of the Industrial Revolution but the working conditions for miners were bad. In Scotland, until 1799, some coalminers were like slaves, bought and sold by coal-mine owners. Before 1842, men, women and children as young as five worked underground in coal mines all over Britain. Coal mines were dangerous places where roofs sometimes caved in, explosions and floods were likely and workers got all sorts of injuries. There were very few safety rules. Later, in the nineteenth century, new safety laws and advances in technology led to improvements in mining. However, although coalmining became safer, it was never really that safe.

By the end of this chapter you should be able to:

▸ Explain why more coal was needed for the Industrial Revolution.
▸ Describe the working conditions of coalminers.
▸ Describe how coalmining became safer but was never completely safe by 1900.

Was coalmining invented for the Industrial Revolution?

Coal had been mined in Britain for hundreds of years before 1760. As far back as 1291, monks in Dunfermline were given the right to open a bell-pit mine. The first coal used was probably found washed up on seashores, and early coal mines were fairly shallow. It is likely that someone had found an outcrop of coal on the surface and had dug down to the coal **seam**.

> **GLOSSARY**
> **Seam** a layer of underground coal that miners cut into
> **Pit** a coal mine

What is a coal seam?

Imagine a cake with several layers. There might be a top layer of sponge, then a layer of cream, then jam, then ice cream, then sponge again.

If you wanted to poke down from the top to get the ice cream you would have to go through the layers and stop once you had got to the ice cream layer. That is how people mined for coal. Coal is under different layers of earth and there are more layers of rock beneath. The bell **pit** was dug down into the coal seam but no further. The miners then dug into the side of the seam, but there was a problem. If they dug out too far, then the rocks above would fall down. Bell pits were fine as long as not too much coal was needed.

What was coalmining in Britain like in 1760?

Mining around 1760 was very basic. Technology had not been invented to allow deep underground mining. Mining still used the old bell-pit idea or adit mines.

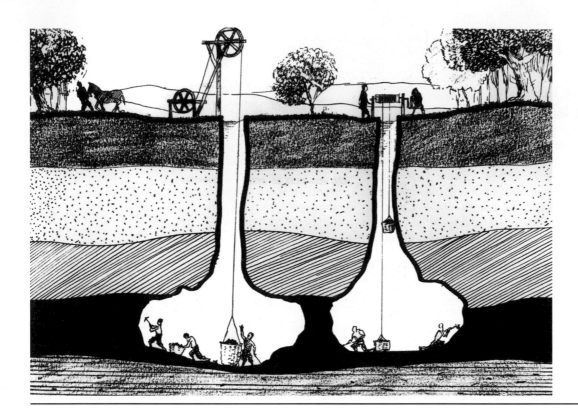

A drawing of a bell pit.

A bell pit was a vertical shaft dug into the ground. Miners were either lowered down by a rope or climbed down a ladder. They started digging outwards into the rocks looking for the coal seam. This sort of pit was like a bell in shape, hence the name.

Bell pits were very dangerous. Water collected at the bottom of the pit and it would soon fill up. Water pumps had to empty the pits before the miners could get to work. The roofs of the bell pits were always unstable and there were no attempts made to **prop** them up with wooden beams. It meant that cave-ins were common. After a short time in use, bell pits had to be abandoned and another pit started close by near the coal seam. It was a very inefficient way of mining coal.

> **GLOSSARY**
> **Prop** a beam or support to hold something up

Adit pits were more successful and slightly safer than bell pits. Adit pits were really just tunnels cut into the side of hills where coal was known to exist. At first, the tunnels were very short but later they would be deepened and wooden props were used to support the roof, making them more stable. If you have visited the coal mine at Beamish Museum in County Durham then you have been in an adit pit.

Adit pits had their own problems. For example, you could only use them where there were coal seams that could be mined into from the sides of hills. Also, the deeper the tunnel went into the side of the hill, the harder it became for miners to get fresh air to breathe.

Why did mines get bigger and deeper after 1760?

After 1760 there was an enormous increase in the demand for coal. Although coal was used as the main fuel in the fireplaces of thousands of homes, there were many other uses for coal and that meant more was needed.

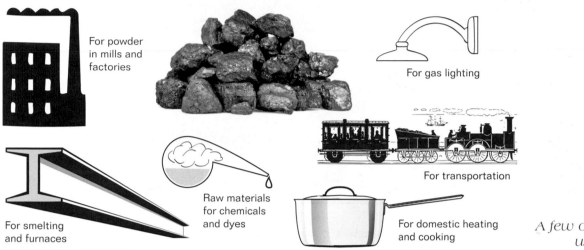

For powder in mills and factories

For gas lighting

For smelting and furnaces

Raw materials for chemicals and dyes

For transportation

For domestic heating and cooking

A few of the many uses of coal.

Coal was the fuel of the Industrial Revolution and as demand grew, miners had to dig more coal. Once a load of coal has been taken out of a mine it can never be replaced. To get more coal, miners had to dig deeper.

What were conditions like in coal mines?

Work in coal mines was often dangerous, and because the whole family was often employed, it was a danger that was shared between parents and children. Coalminers lived and worked in small communities near the mine. Miners only received money for the coal they dug once it reached the surface, so mining became a family operation with men cutting the coal below ground and the wives and children carrying the coal to the surface.

If there was a sudden emergency such as an explosion or a flood, what problems would miners face getting out of this pit?

This drawing shows a small section of the Gilmerton coal mine near Edinburgh. Look at the different levels of mining work. They are called galleries. Look at how the galleries are connected. The only exit from the pit is way above the top of the drawing. Remember this picture only shows a small section of a coal mine.

Hewers were the miners who actually cut or 'hewed' the coal from the seam of rock. Adult men or older boys worked as hewers, cutting and digging coal using a pick and shovel, often in very cramped conditions. Hewers might have to stoop or even lie on their sides to get at the coal, depending on how tall the mine seam was. After all, there was no point – and no money – in digging out rock.

If you were a hewer, what do you think would happen to your body after years of this work?

A coal hewer at work.

Bearers were often mothers and older daughters who carried or dragged baskets of coal either to the surface or to the winch that lifted the coal to the surface. The work was heavy, exhausting and back breaking. In some mines, women and children would have to carry the coal up the spiralling walkway to the surface, or up the ladders connecting different levels in the mines.

A woman carrying coal.

Two women carrying coal up a ladder.

Putters were young children who filled the tubs and baskets with coal and then pushed or dragged them before the coal was carried to the surface by bearers.

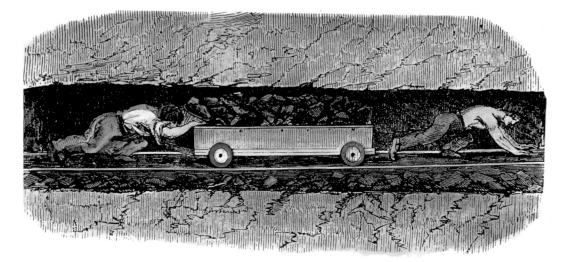

Children moving coal to a mine's surface.

As mines became deeper, the dangers from the lack of breathable air became readily apparent. One way of improving this was the use of trappers to open and close doors in the mines.

Trappers were very young children, too young or too weak to work as bearers, who opened and shut **ventilation** doors when carts had passed. This closed off the air flow to some areas of the mine while increasing the amount of air in others. Some trappers were only five or six years old. They worked 12 hours each day.

GLOSSARY

Ventilation getting air into the mine to allow miners to breathe

Why did workers put up with the conditions shown here and in the previous illustrations?

A trapper opening a ventilation door to allow a pair of putters to pass with their coal.

What dangers did miners face underground?

Ever since the first miner went underground to cut coal, mining has been a hard and dangerous job. Mines were dark, damp and dangerous. Serious accidents and falls were common and there were many dangers present in coal mines:

Miners always faced the risk of drowning in a flood, gas explosions, cave-ins or invisible gas that killed by suffocation.

Coalmining became even more dangerous after 1760 as the increased demand for coal meant that miners had to work deeper underground.

The build-up of gas underground was a very serious threat to safety. **Fire damp** was a mixture of methane gas, which leaked from the coal, and stale air. The gas was extremely explosive, and would ignite when it was exposed to open flames. Around 1760, miners used ordinary candles to light their way, and that could set off an explosion. To get around this, many miners chose to work in the dark, which was a lonely and dangerous situation. Some miners even took rotting fish down the mine with them. When some types of fish rot they glow with a dim luminous light. Miners used that glow to see as they cut into a seam.

Choke damp, also known as black damp, killed by suffocation. It had no smell but suffocated miners. They felt drowsy, fell asleep and died. Choke damp gas reduced oxygen in the air to a point that life could not exist because other gases replaced the oxygen. That's why miners took canaries into gassy pits. Canaries have smaller lungs than humans and they would die quickly when oxygen levels fell. Miners knew that when the birds fell silent – or just fell! – then they had just minutes to get out of the mine.

Miners often suffered from long-term health problems such as black lung or the black spit; the medical name is pneumoconiosis. Black lung was a nasty disease caused by a long-term exposure to coal dust. Miners would breathe the dust into their lungs where it would accumulate. The effects were similar to the long-term effect of smoking tobacco in that it destroyed the miners' lungs.

Deformity and wasting: children who worked long hours in damp, cramped conditions often grew up deformed and would die at a young age.

Falls: miners were lowered into pits on ropes. The ropes could snap or the turning handle slip and miners could fall to their deaths. In some pits, coal was carried up rotting slippery wooden steps. There were few safety checks on ladders or ropes.

Drowning: if a pit flooded, miners could drown.

Crushing: roof falls could trap and kill miners.

Suffocation and explosion: poisonous gases could cause death or could explode, killing miners.

Some of the dangers faced by coalminers.

GLOSSARY

Fire damp an explosive gas

Choke damp a mixture of gases that remove oxygen from the air

Did new technology improve the working conditions of the miners?

In the nineteenth century, new technology helped to reduce some of the dangers in mines.

▶ Steam pumps drained water from mines and winding engines with wire cables and cages reduced the risks when being lowered into and raised from the pit.
▶ Pit props lessened the risk of cave-ins.
▶ Ventilation fans pushed fresh air around a mine.
▶ The Davy lamp reduced the risks of explosions by preventing naked flames coming into contact with explosive gases underground.

By 1900, new mechanical cutters and conveyor belts were being used in British mines. These did increase coal production but often caused new safety problems such as even more dust and very dangerous moving parts.

By looking at the picture, how would you answer the claim that the Davy safety lamp made mining much easier?

Miners working by the light of a Davy lamp.

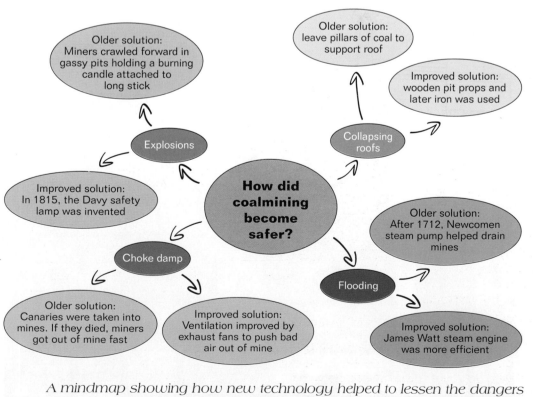

Older solution: Miners crawled forward in gassy pits holding a burning candle attached to long stick

Explosions

Improved solution: In 1815, the Davy safety lamp was invented

Choke damp

Older solution: Canaries were taken into mines. If they died, miners got out of mine fast

Improved solution: Ventilation improved by exhaust fans to push bad air out of mine

How did coalmining become safer?

Older solution: leave pillars of coal to support roof

Improved solution: wooden pit props and later iron was used

Collapsing roofs

Older solution: After 1712, Newcomen steam pump helped drain mines

Flooding

Improved solution: James Watt steam engine was more efficient

A mindmap showing how new technology helped to lessen the dangers in coal mines.

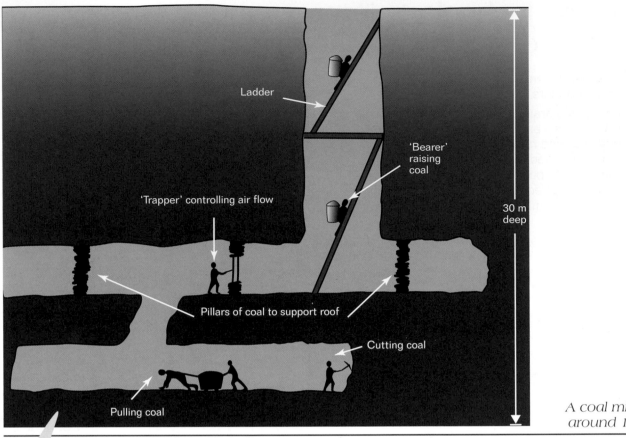

Ladder

'Bearer' raising coal

'Trapper' controlling air flow

30 m deep

Pillars of coal to support roof

Cutting coal

Pulling coal

A coal mine in around 1800.

In what ways do the two drawings show how safety in mines improved but at the same time the dangers increased? Aim for at least six improvements but also one thing that might make mines more dangerous.

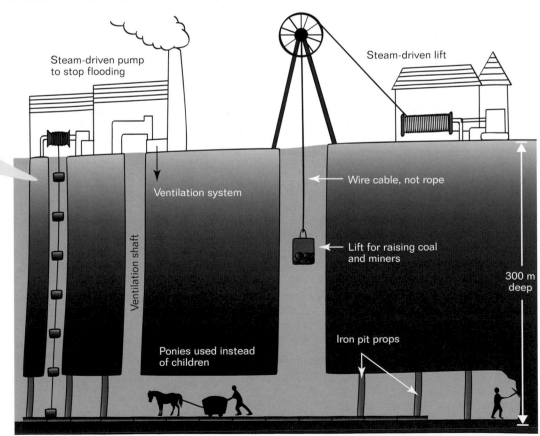

Steam-driven pump to stop flooding

Steam-driven lift

Ventilation system

Ventilation shaft

Wire cable, not rope

Lift for raising coal and miners

Ponies used instead of children

Iron pit props

300 m deep

A coal mine in around 1900.

In what ways did new technology make things worse?

There were some obvious improvements in safety in the mines, particularly with the introduction of pit props and water pumps. However, they did not eliminate the dangers of cave-ins and floods. They just improved the odds of survival.

It is also true that new technology even increased the risks since mines could get bigger and deeper. In almost every mine, accidents were an everyday occurrence. Even the new Davy lamp did not stop all explosions. In 1877, for example, 200 men in Blantyre were killed by an explosion that was caused by a naked flame. The new technology meant improvements in coal production but not necessarily improvements in miner safety.

Did new laws improve working conditions in mines?

Between 1842 and 1900 there were several important new laws designed to help improve miners' working conditions. The public had been shocked by the deaths of 26 children in a flash flood at a mine in Silkstone near Barnsley in 1838 and pressure mounted on the government to do something about children in the mines.

In 1840, the government set up a **Royal Commission** to investigate conditions in coal mines. The commissioners visited mines across the country, taking notes about how they were run, who was employed, their ages and working conditions. A lot of mine owners were not happy to see the commissioners, and tried to refuse them entry.

> **GLOSSARY**
> **Royal Commission** an investigation set up by the government

What did the commission's report show?

The commission reported in 1842 and published a detailed report, *The First Report of the Children's Employment Commissioners*. The report revealed the horrible conditions that young children and women had to cope with in mines. The investigation collected evidence from men, women and children and made comments such as the following:

Janet Cummings, 11 years old. *Works with father. Has done for two years. Father gangs [goes to work] at two in the morning. Janet said, 'I gang with the women at five in the morning and come up at five at night. I work all Friday night and come up at 12 on Saturday morning. I carry large bits of coal from the wall face to the pit bottom in a creel on my back. The roof is very low and I have to bend my back and legs and the water comes up my legs. I don't like the work but I must do it.*

Robert Drury, 10 years old. *I trap in the pit. I don't like it because it's in the dark. I go sometimes at six in the morning; on Saturdays I go at five and come out after six in the evening. They use me well in the pit, they never beat me.*

Ann Hague, 13 years old. *I hurry [chained to heavy carts of coal and pull the carts to the pit surface]. There is a little girl, my sister, who pushes behind. We go at six in the morning and come away at two in the afternoon. We have our breakfast before we go, and take our dinner with us and get it when we can at the pit: when we've a minute to spare. We often stop as much as half an hour. I don't like working in the pit so very well. I would rather not do it.*

Of all the pictures drawn showing the horrible working conditions, this is the picture that shocked so many people at the time. Use Google Images to search for '1842 Mines Act' to see more of the pictures drawn by the investigators.

Children being lowered into a pit by a woman using a winch.

Artists also drew accurate illustrations showing what conditions were like. The drawings also carried many pictures of young girls working bare-breasted close to men. This horrified some Victorians even more than the terrible working conditions.

The report of the Royal Commission caused such an outcry that it was inevitable there would be demands for new laws to improve conditions in coal mines.

What did the 1842 Mines Act do to improve working conditions?

The act of 1842 focused mainly on the conditions of women and children. The law stated that:

▶ No women should work underground.
▶ Children under ten were not allowed to work underground.
▶ No one under the age of 15 was to be in charge of moving machinery or operating the winch that lowered people into the mines or lifted them out.
▶ Ponies were to drag the coal underground.

How important was the 1842 Mines Act?

At first glance the 1842 act seemed to be a massive step forward in improving the conditions of women and children working in the mining industry, but it had limited success. To begin with, there was only one **inspector** to enforce the law in all of Britain and Ireland – and even then the inspector was not allowed to go underground! Mine owners felt they could safely ignore the rules – and many working women were only too happy to break the rules too!

> **GLOSSARY**
>
> **Inspector** a person who had the job of checking that mines were following the law
>
> **Precedent** a guide for future action

The act didn't stop girls and women from being employed by the mine owners; they just couldn't work underground. Instead, they did lots of heavy, dirty and dangerous work above ground. They did not want to be stopped working underground because these jobs were better paid. Women and children could still work above ground but they were paid less for surface work such as sorting and bagging coal.

It was also very difficult for the inspector to check the ages of children working in mines. There were no regular recordings of births before 1837, so it was hard to say exactly how old the children were and anyway, their parents usually lied about their ages. This was because their parents worked in the mines themselves. They had no childcare and believed that their children would be better off working and earning money for the family. Many parents actually hated the act and sided with the mine owners. As a result, hardly any of the mine owners obeyed the act.

Finally, the act did nothing to help the hours worked by adult men. They were still working long shifts underground, perhaps as long as 11 or 12 hours. It was still not unknown for miners in some pits to be underground for 24 hours.

Was the 1842 Mines Act a failure?

Looking at the list of problems with the act, you might be forgiven for thinking it was a failure, but some historians believe that it was a useful first phase in changing the conditions of miners. It did take the important step of appointing an inspector, even though he didn't really have many powers to enforce the law. The most important thing the act did was to set a **precedent**. That is, the government had made a start in improving conditions in coal mines and they could do so again.

What was the 1850 Coal Mines Inspections Act?

In 1850, a new act passed by parliament seemed to deal with some of the problems left over from the 1842 act. First, the government realised it needed more inspectors and more were hired. Then, the government gave the inspectors the power to insist that they could go underground, even if the mine owner had forbidden it. The inspectors could now write real reports on the conditions at the mines. They were also given powers to enforce the rules set out in the 1842 act, and to make sure mines were as safe as they could be. It also became compulsory for mine owners to report all accidents that led to a death. For the first time, the government could keep track of how many people were actually dying in the mines.

Did the 1850 act change anything?

For the first time, mine owners could be prosecuted in the courts if they broke the 1842 act. Unfortunately there were very few prosecutions so many mine owners did still get away with not caring about their workers.

What other laws helped to improve the conditions of the miners?

Between 1855 and 1900, a series of laws continued to improve the working conditions of the workers underground. These included:

▶ The 1855 Mines Act stated that each mine now had to have its own set of safety rules. These plans had to be shown to the government and approved by law.

▶ The 1860 Mines Regulation and Inspection Act introduced more safety rules for the new technologies that were being used in the mines. It also increased the numbers of mine inspectors employed by the government. The act also increased the age of boys that were allowed to work underground to 12. Anyone under that age was no longer allowed to work in the mines.

▶ The 1862 Mines Act made single mine shafts illegal. Mines now had to have two exits, rather than just one. This meant that if there was a tunnel collapse to the main entrance, the miners would not be trapped underground. As an added bonus this also helped to increase ventilation in the mines, further improving the safety conditions.

▶ The 1872 Coal Mines Regulating Act made it compulsory for mine owners to have a certificate of **competency**. This certificate was awarded to the owners or their managers after passing a national exam. It was the first time that mine owners had to prove that they were fit and able to run such dangerous businesses. The act also made attempts to improve the safety conditions in each of the mines:

> **GLOSSARY**
>
> **Competency** the ability to do something properly

    – Fans had to be installed to improve ventilation.

    – Pit props had to be made from strong timber or steel.

    – All mines had to use safety lamps; naked flames were now forbidden.

    – Winches were to be fitted with improved winding gears, to prevent them from accidentally slipping and dropping coal or people back down into the pits.

    – Finally, and most importantly, miners were able to appoint their own safety inspectors. These inspectors would have a much better knowledge of the mines and be able to spot any safety concerns and report them to a national inspector.

How successful were the new laws?

By the end of the nineteenth century, mines had never been safer but there were still well over 1000 recorded deaths a year in British coal mines.

New technology could only do so much to provide protection for the miners and reduce the number of accidents. One reason it was less effective was because coal-mine owners did not want to spend large amounts of money on improvements.

The new laws were successful in preventing young children from being exploited underground, boys and women were forbidden from working underground and, by 1900, there was a set number of hours to the working day for all men.

How important was the coal industry in 1900?

By 1900, coal mines were producing more coal than ever before. The number of miners continued to increase. In 1850, there were around 200,000 miners but by 1900 the number was well over a million. Coal production also increased. In 1830, almost 16 million tons of coal had been dug up out of the pits. By 1900 that amount had increased to over 250 million tons.

How would you answer the claim that the Industrial Revolution in Britain was built on the graves of the workers who died getting the fuel to make it happen?

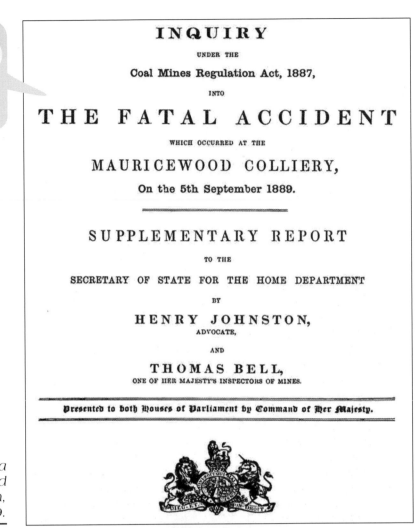

The title page of the report into a fatal accident at the Mauricewood coal mine at Penicuik, Midlothian, in 1889.

Activity 1

Numeracy counts

Design two different, colourful and annotated charts or graphs to show the changes in employment and production in the coal industry during the nineteenth century.

Activity 2

Summarise this chapter

The following summary reminds you of what this chapter has been about. Words that are important have been made into ANAGRAMS. Your task is to sort out the anagrams and then write the correct version of this summary into your workbook or work file.

The fuel of the Industrial Revolution was **LOAC**. As demand increased for more and more coal, the **SMINE LOAC** got **PERDEE**. As miners dug further into the ground **GERSDAN** increased such as **FOOR LFALL, SAG** explosions and **DINGFLOO**. Working conditions in the mines were very harsh. Men were **WERSHE**, women and older girls who carried the coal were **RERSBEA** while very young children who opened and shut trap doors to improve **LITAVENTION** were called **ERSTRAPP**. In **2491** a **SMINE TCA** improved conditions. Children under **NET** were not allowed underground and neither were any **MENOW**. Other acts improved working conditions and technology improved safety but even by 1900 coal mines were **FERSA** but were never **EFSA**.

Activity 3

Cartoon analysis

By 1900, change was on its way for the coal industry. This cartoon from around 1900 shows 'King Coal' and 'King Steam' looking at a new baby – electricity.

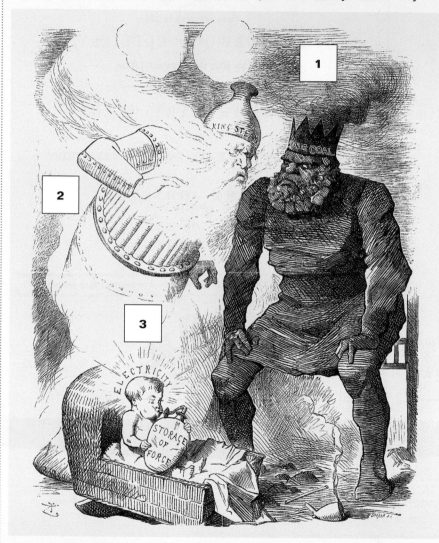

"What will he grow to?"

The cartoon has been labelled with numbers. Describe exactly what you see in the picture at the points numbered 1–3.

▶ Why are figures 1 and 2 looking worried?
▶ Why is figure 3 shown as a baby?
▶ You know that electricity did grow to become very important in everyone's lives. Was this cartoon prophetic (a word that means able to tell the future)?

Activity 4

Design a poster

Use the information in this chapter or the previous one and your own knowledge to design an information poster.

The information poster should show:

▶ How either the cotton or the coal industry changed between 1760 and 1900.
▶ Why either the cotton or the coal industry changed between 1760 and 1900.

There are a variety of ways you can design this. A few ideas are listed below:

▶ You could present the information in the form of a leaflet, a mindmap or a storyboard that shows the changes in the industries.

▶ There may also be an opportunity for you to design a slideshow presentation that can be shared with the class or shown on your school's website for revision.
▶ You can produce your own images or you can print off images from the internet to cut out and stick on your information poster to make a collage.

Your information poster should do the following:

▶ Describe how the coal or cotton industry changed.
▶ Explain why the industry changed.
▶ What do you think was the main reason why your chosen industry changed so much? Explain your answer in your poster.

Question practice

National 4

Source A is from the report of the Royal Commission set up in 1840 to investigate conditions in coal mines.

SOURCE A

We have reports of terrible working conditions in the coal mines of East Lothian. In one case a pregnant woman had to pull a coal truck with a belt strapped round her waist as she crawled in darkness underground. She gave birth in the mine but was not allowed to surface with the child until the end of her shift. The baby died.

Describe in your own words the working conditions in coal mines before 1842. You should use Source A and your own knowledge.

Success criteria

Include at least two factual points of information, or one developed piece of information, about working conditions in coal mines.

National 5

This is a 'describe' question. In this type of question you will be asked to describe either what happened or the effects of an event or a development.

Describe the impact of new technology on coalmining in the nineteenth century. (6 marks)

To be successful you need to give five or six pieces of accurate recall. These could include steam-powered machinery for pumping water or improvements to ventilation or the use of mechanical cage lifts. You can always gain an additional mark if you bring in more information to back up a point you are making, such as 'More steam-powered machinery was used for pumping water [1 mark]. This reduced the risk of flooding, which had always been a problem when miners went deeper underground [1 extra mark].'

Transport – canals and railways

3

Chapter 7 Canals

What is this chapter about?

A big problem in the early Industrial Revolution was how to carry heavy, bulky things such as iron and coal and also fragile things such as pottery goods from where they were made to where they would be sold. Roads at the time were not suitable; they were slow, dangerous and full of potholes. An early solution to Britain's transport problem was canals. Canals spread across Britain in the eighteenth century but they were not the answer to all transport problems. Canals were expensive and difficult to build and travelling along them was slow. Eventually canals became less important as railways were developed.

By the end of this chapter you should be able to:

▶ Explain why transport improvements were necessary for the Industrial Revolution to happen.
▶ Describe the advantages and disadvantages of canals as a means of transport.

Why transport had to improve

When the Industrial Revolution started in Britain it was vital to have good communications. Businesspeople had to travel around the country safely and efficiently. In 1760, the coach service took 12 days to travel between Edinburgh and London and only made the journey once every two weeks. There wasn't even a service between London and Glasgow.

As new industries in Britain began to develop after 1760, they needed coal and iron in large amounts. One of the most serious problems that had to be overcome was the difficulty of carrying these heavy and bulky materials around the country.

The road system was in poor condition, often no more than dirt tracks that could become impassable in the winter. Moving coal and iron needed large numbers of packhorses or wagons and this was very slow and expensive.

From 1760, the Industrial Revolution in Britain required that transport improve. Raw materials had to be taken to factories. Often these were big and bulky such as bales of raw cotton. Steam engines needed large amounts of coal to produce their power. Stone was needed for new buildings. Iron was also needed in large amounts. Industry

This is the type of wagon that would have transported goods around Britain before the Industrial Revolution.

also produced **fragile** things such as precision-made tools and pottery – things that were easily damaged or broken on rough bumpy roads. The Industrial Revolution depended on efficient transport – something that Britain did not have in 1760.

Roads were simply not suitable. It was a lot of hard work to transport enough food into major cities just to keep the population fed. Horses struggled to carry or pull bags and wagons loaded with all the things a city needed. The new industries and factories requiring plentiful supplies of coal, iron, cotton and chemicals added another burden to the road network.

Transporting heavy goods by boat was easier. Coastal ships were often used to carry coal. Most of the coal used in London was shipped by sea from Newcastle. Towards the end of the eighteenth century almost all of the growing industrial centres developed near waterways. The major rivers became highways for commercial goods and were much more important than roads. However, there was a problem: not all coalfields or industries were near to the coast. Rivers were also used to move coal and iron but again there was a problem because not all parts of the country had rivers that were deep enough for boats.

The first answer to Britain's transport problem was canals. It was far easier to transport heavy loads on **barges** pulled by horses along 'water motorways'.

GLOSSARY

Fragile easily broken

Barges long flat-bottomed boats pulled along canals by horses

The spread of canals across Britain in the eighteenth century

The first modern canal in Britain was the Bridgewater Canal, opened in 1761. The canal was used to carry coal from the Duke of Bridgewater's coal mines to the growing industrial city of Manchester. Later, the canal was extended to Liverpool to carry cotton.

A barge being pulled along a canal by a horse.

Was carrying goods by canal really faster than road transport? Think carefully about your answer.

The Duke of Bridgewater was a rich and powerful man who owned coal mines in north-west England. The growth of the city of Manchester meant an increase in the demand for his coal. The problem was how to get the coal to Manchester quickly and in bulk. The old route of using two rivers, the Mersey and the Irwell, was too slow for the Duke's needs. It was also taking too long to transport the coal by packhorses to the Mersey. The cost of the journey meant that the Duke's coal was not as profitable as it could be. The Duke hired an engineer called James Brindley to build a canal and oversee the project. The canal Brindley built from the coal mines to Manchester, where there were purpose-built warehouses ready to receive the barges, cost £168,000.

So impressive was the Bridgewater Canal's construction that it became an instant tourist attraction and people from all over Britain came just to see it. When the canal opened in 1761, it immediately proved to be a commercial success. Barges carrying 30 tons of coal quickly began to arrive in Manchester. Within a few years the cost of coal had halved.

The Bridgewater Canal had been so successful that other businesspeople began to develop plans for canals in their own areas. For example, the Grand Trunk Canal was the brainchild of leading pottery businessman Josiah Wedgwood. Wedgwood had a thriving pottery business but needed to link his potteries in Stoke-on-Trent to the docks of Liverpool, to make it easier to sell his products. He had seen the success of the Bridgewater Canal and realised how important it was to transport his products rapidly and smoothly so as to avoid breakages.

In Scotland, canals were developed from the 1760s. The most important focus in canal building was on the Clyde, where major manufacturing in shipbuilding led to the need for more transportation. By 1791, the east and west were connected, as the River Clyde was joined to the River Forth by a series of canals. The Forth and Clyde Canal carried almost 200,000 passengers by 1812.

> How does this painting illustrate why canals were built and what their advantages were?

The canal shown in this modern painting is beside Wedgwood's factory in an area of England called the Potteries.

What problems were there in building canals?

Canals were very difficult to build. The designers faced a lot of different problems. Canals either had to be kept level or, if the land to be crossed was hilly, a series of **locks** had to be built. Locks were like 'steps of water' that canal barges had to go up and down, one 'step' at a time while water levels were lowered or raised.

If canals were to be kept level, then tunnels or ways of carrying the canals over valleys, using **aqueducts**, had to be built.

Not everyone wanted to sell their land to canal companies and those that did often demanded a higher price than it was worth. There were also compensation claims from the owners of wagons and packhorses who lost their livelihoods when the canals were opened.

The canals had to be filled with water and they needed a constant supply in order to keep them at the right level. This meant that reservoirs had to be built and pumping stations were required to supply the water.

> ### GLOSSARY
>
> **Locks** a way of raising barges up and down a series of 'steps' to allow canal traffic to cope with hilly ground
>
> **Aqueducts** water-filled bridges that allow boats to pass over valleys

Who built the canals?

To build canals, thousands of men were needed to dig out earth and stones. It was hard and dangerous physical labour, using only basic tools and equipment: picks, spades and wheelbarrows.

Canals allowed boats to travel, or navigate, across areas of Britain away from the rivers or coast. The canal diggers were called inland navigators. The name was soon shorted to **navvies**.

GLOSSARY

Navvies the labourers who built canals

Canal mania a craze to invest money in building new canals, hoping to make big profits

At first, the problem was how to find enough workers to dig all these canals at the same time. The answer to this shortage of workers was to bring unemployed men from Ireland or the Highlands of Scotland. Both these groups of people were leaving their homelands because of hunger and poverty and were looking for work in the industrial areas of Britain.

The navvies were low paid, lived in very poor conditions and at times were treated harshly by the foremen in charge of their jobs. Navvies worked in gangs in all weathers and lived in tents or rough shelters near the canals they were digging. Villagers near to the canal-building works would be afraid when they heard navvies were arriving – as they had a reputation for being heavy drinkers and hard fighters – but the villagers also wanted the benefits of having a canal nearby.

Why were canals so popular?

Canals were popular because they provided a better system of transport. By the 1860s, almost 8000 km of canals had been built in Britain. The canals helped British industry to develop by providing a cheap means of transport, allowing raw materials to arrive at factories and manufactured products to be taken to waiting ships to be sold around the world.

Canals reduced the cost of transporting coal, which led to cheaper coal in towns. The same was true of iron, cotton and other goods carried to and from factories. Quarries could use the canals to transport large quantities of stone to ports to be shipped around the world. The network of inland canals that had been created allowed farmers to send their crops to distant markets and to bring in large amounts of fertiliser and lime to improve crop yields.

The canals were especially useful in transporting fragile, easily breakable goods such as pottery. Previously, packhorses, wagons and carts would have led to many more breakages.

Canals were a big help to the British economy. Thousands of workers were employed to build the canals, but the effects on other industries were huge and the boost to the economy cannot be underestimated.

What was 'canal mania'?

Canals made money for those who had invested in them. As canals became even more successful, investors rushed to pour money into building canals, hoping for a share in the profits.

Between 1790 and 1796, parliament passed acts authorising the construction of 122 new canals. When a new canal was announced, investors would rush to the meetings hoping to buy shares. Many investors then immediately resold the shares for a quick profit. It became such a mad rush that meetings about new canals were held in secret to avoid rioting investors turning up.

This was the time of the craze for canals and it was called '**canal mania**'. Everybody wanted to get rich by sharing in the profits of canals. By the 1790s there were so many canals being built that some of them were completely unnecessary but still investors wanted to pour money into them.

Why did canals become less important?

It is often said that canals started to become less important when the railways were invented. While that is partly true, it is an exaggeration. At first, the canal owners were not overly worried about the advance of the railways. Their business was already well established, and many thought that it would be impossible for the steam locomotives to be able to haul enough cargo to make a difference to their profits.

Canal barges were not the fastest mode of transport available. The average speed of a fully loaded barge was only about 5 km/hour, roughly the walking speed of an adult human. In the eighteenth century this was considered a fast way of moving goods inland, but by the nineteenth century it was beginning to look out of date.

So what possible reasons were there for the decline of the canals, other than the development of the railways?

How important was the lack of maintenance of canals?

Canal owners had never been particularly keen on spending their profits on maintaining the canals.

Canal locks needed constant maintenance or they would begin to deteriorate. As canals began to look shabby, people lost confidence in them, the canal banks became muddy, and the barges were unable to carry full loads. In summer, some canals started to dry out while in the winter the canals often froze over. Customers began to look for different ways to move their goods.

A derelict canal.

Try to estimate roughly when this picture was taken. What do you think occurred to result in this happening to the canal?

Did canals disappear completely?

By 1900, some canals were still being used and were still making a profit. The Bridgewater Canal, for example, continued to make a profit between Liverpool and Manchester, despite the competing railway line.

In 1891 the Manchester Ship Canal was opened, giving Manchester direct access to the sea for the first time. It meant that the city's merchants no longer had to pay the massive fares for shipping goods by train to Liverpool's docks. The merchants also avoided the dock charges there.

Some canals were even saved by a new fashion – tourism. The 1870s saw a revival of interest in the canal network. Newspapers ran campaigns to save canals and this drew a lot of attention from the public.

The first book on travelling the waterways was published in 1896, by J.B. Dashwood. This sparked a new wave of pleasure trips on barges along Britain's canals. Can it be argued that canals and **narrowboats** are still serving British industry even today?

> **GLOSSARY**
>
> **Narrowboats** self-powered boats for use on canals, similar to barges

Narrowboat holiday.

Activity 1

Summarise this chapter

The following summary reminds you of what this chapter has been about. Words that are important have been made into ANAGRAMS. Your task is to sort out the anagrams and then write the correct version of this summary into your workbook or work file.

*Once the Industrial Revolution started it was clear that Britain needed much better **POTRTRANS**. The old **OADSR** were totally unsuitable to carry heavy, bulky things such as **LOAC** and **ILEFRAG** things such as **OTTERYP**. In 1760, the answer to the problem seemed to be **CLANAS** but they were not the answer to all transport problems. The first canal to help supply coal was the **WATERBRIDGE** canal that took coal to **CHESTERMAN**. Canals were built by **VVIESAN**. There were only a few canals built in Scotland, partly because of the difficulty of building in such **ILLYH** areas. Canals were also slow. Canals became less important when **WAYRAILS** spread over Britain in the mid-nineteenth century.*

Activity 2

The challenge! How far can you go?

The following questions go up in level of difficulty in pairs. The first two are easy. The last two are hard. How many will you try to do?

1. What was the first modern canal in Britain called?
2. Who was James Brindley?

3. Why did industrialisation lead to the development of canals?
4. Since railways were more useful and caused canals to become less popular, why do you think businesspeople did not just build railways first and not bother with canals?

5. Just by looking at the pictures in this chapter, what conclusions can you reach about the importance of canals between 1760 and 1800?
6. If you wanted to start a 'green' eco-friendly business today, would you consider the use of canals – including building one? What factors would influence your decision? Apply your thoughts and decisions to the time around 1760. Which of your reasons would still apply then and which would not? Why not?

Activity 3

Prepare a presentation

▶ Find out some information about a canal. Try to choose the one that is nearest to your town.
▶ Present your findings in an attractive and mature way. How you choose to present them is up to you.

The following core questions must be answered:

▶ What is the canal called?
▶ When was it built?
▶ Why was it built?

You should also find old photos, caption them and take new ones yourself, explaining your reason for taking them. Include the story of your canal with information about its life. Negotiate how much time you can spend on this with your teacher.

Question practice

National 4

Source A is adapted from a newspaper report written by H. Neale, a journalist reporting about transport changes in 1800.

SOURCE A

Canals have changed this nation so much since I was a boy. Now I can eat food brought from the sea ports 50 miles [80 km] away. I can send fragile things to another town and they arrive undamaged. The old road owners complain about canals but that is only because they can no longer charge us so much to use overgrown tracks filled with potholes that they call roads!

Describe in your own words some of the things that happened to people in Britain when canals were built nearby. You should use Source A and your own knowledge.

Success criteria

Include at least two factual points of information, or one developed piece of information, about the effects of canal transport. You can write about the good things and the bad things if you want to.

National 5

Source A is from *The Journey from Chester to London* written by Thomas Pennant in 1782.

SOURCE A

The cottage instead of being half covered by thatch is now covered with a substantial cover of tiles or slates, brought from the distant hills of Wales or Cumberland. The fields, which before were barren, are now drained and by the assistance of manure, clothed with beautiful greenness. Places which rarely knew the use of coal are plentifully supplied with it at reasonable prices. And what is of still greater public benefit, corn merchants are prevented from charging high prices by the availability of cheaper competition.

Evaluate the usefulness of Source A as evidence of the effects of canals on economy and society in Britain after 1760. You may want to comment on who wrote it, when they wrote it, why they wrote it, what they say or what has been missed out. (6 marks)

Success criteria

- To get 1 mark, you need to explain the importance of each of the points you make about the source.
- Up to 4 marks may be given for evaluative comments about origin and purpose. Comments about the origin may include an explanation about the type of source, the author or the timing of the source. Comments about purpose may include an explanation about why the source was written.
- Up to 2 marks may be given for your evaluation of the content of the source which you consider is useful in terms of the proposed question. For full marks to be given, each point needs to be discretely mentioned and its usefulness explained.
- If you list information, it will be considered to be one point and will get only 1 mark.
- Up to 2 marks may be given for evaluative comments relating to points of information not mentioned in the source.

Chapter 8 Railways

What is this chapter about?

Railways started to replace canals by the 1830s. By the 1850s, gangs of navvies worked across Britain building a network of rail lines connecting Britain's towns and industrial areas. By the end of the nineteenth century almost every village in Britain was connected. At first there was some opposition to railways but people who were against railways were ignored when the benefits became obvious. Railways provided a better means of transport around Britain. Railways provided tens of thousands of new jobs and changed the way people led their lives. The railways changed Britain forever.

By the end of this chapter you should be able to:

▶ Explain why railways had such a big effect on Britain's society and economy.
▶ Describe the development of railways in the nineteenth century.

Why were railways needed?

At the start of the nineteenth century, transport in Britain was based on roads, canals and **coastal shipping**. If industry was to continue to grow, a better system of moving things around was needed which could provide reliable, fast transport for passengers and goods.

What was a 'railway' in 1800?

To most people the word 'railway' means an engine moving on wheels and pulling carriages. The earliest railways were just wagons on wooden rails used to carry coal short distances downhill to rivers or coasts. By 1700, coal mines in Tranent were linked with Port Seton harbour by wooden trackways. Iron rails started to become more common by the second half of the eighteenth century and horses were used to pull the wagons. Longer railway tracks were laid down and horse-drawn wagons were a common sight by the 1820s. By 1810, there were about 500 km of such trackways.

> Is this illustration an effective way of showing why railways were developed and used in the 1700s and early 1800s? Does it show how the early trackways operated?

Horses hauling coal.

> **GLOSSARY**
>
> **Coastal shipping** ships that carried goods between coastal towns and on main rivers

How did steam-powered railways start?

Steam engines had been invented in the 1700s and by 1800 people knew how to make steam engines turn wheels. Steam was the modern power source. Once a water boiler was developed that could release steam power to move a piston and turn wheels, the uses were almost unlimited. All that was needed was a supply of water, coal to burn and the technology to make it work.

Some steam engines were stationary (they did not move position) and operated long chains or ropes to pull carts and wagons along the rail tracks.

The most famous inventors of the steam **locomotives** were George Stephenson and his son, Robert. George Stephenson was the son of a miner and his first job was working as an engineer in a coal mine. It was there that he invented his first steam-powered locomotive. It pulled 30 tons of coal and impressed the mine owners so much that he was asked to be the chief engineer on the new Stockton to Darlington railway.

> **GLOSSARY**
> **Locomotive** a steam engine that moves under its own power

> Do some research and find out what the six arrows are pointing to and how these parts were vital to the operation of the new steam engines (clue: coal, water, rails and steam were needed). Find YouTube videos of reconstructions showing the 'Rocket' in operation.

1

2

3

4

5

6

Stephenson's 'Rocket'.

When and where did the 'railway age' start?

In the 1830s, railway building began in Britain's industrial areas, especially in the north of England and the Glasgow area.

Stockton to Darlington

Darlington was a coalmining area in north-east England and Stockton was a large port, exporting coal all over Europe. The coal-mine owners wanted an efficient steam engine to pull the coal carts along the Stockton to Darlington route. George Stephenson developed the first reliable steam engine – it was called 'The Locomotion' and the route opened in 1825.

> The text above tells you the purpose of the Stockton to Darlington line. Why does this picture seem odd?

'The Locomotion' on the Stockton to Darlington line.

Liverpool to Manchester

Even during the nineteenth century both Liverpool and Manchester were very important cities in the north of England. Liverpool was a port where large amounts of raw cotton were landed from the USA and the West Indies. Manchester was the centre of a vast network of cotton factories that needed the raw cotton from Liverpool. Both cities depended on each other for their prosperity.

There was a canal between Liverpool and Manchester but its owners charged expensive **tolls** to use the waterway. To get around the canal's tolls it was suggested that a railway might be cheaper. The building of the Liverpool to Manchester line had started in 1824. It took five years to build the railway and cost a huge amount at the time – £740,000 – mainly because of the cost of building a tunnel and 63 bridges to connect the two cities. The cost, in the end, was worth it.

In order to find the right locomotive to run on the line, the Liverpool and Manchester Railway Company held a competition, with the first prize of £500. The competition

> **GLOSSARY**
> **Tolls** money charged to use a road or canal

consisted of race trials between steam locomotives. Only Stephenson's new locomotive – the 'Rocket' – completed the trials, averaging a speed of about 20 km/hour, and so it became the first locomotive working on the Liverpool to Manchester line.

The railway opened on 15 September 1830, and within a month the line was carrying 1200 passengers a day. In its first year the railway carried almost half a million passengers and was a great success. People who had invested in the railway made a fortune.

The amount of profit made by the investors in the Liverpool to Manchester railway caught everyone's imagination. If those investors could make so much money from building a railway between their two cities, then why couldn't investors in other parts of the country make the same amount of money out of new railways where they lived?

What was 'railway mania'?

Britain was gripped by railway mania in the 1830s and 1840s and a network of railway lines soon criss-crossed the country. People hoped to get rich quick by investing their money in new lines, no matter how crazy the plans were. By 1848, when railway mania reached its peak, parliament had agreed to 272 separate new companies building railways. Some towns found themselves with several different lines being built nearby, all connecting the same places. Some lines had no hope of attracting many passengers and some lines had no industry nearby that needed railway transport. Nevertheless, the craze for building railway lines continued.

Who built the railways?

Navvies used picks and shovels to build the railway system. In Chapter 7 you read about the navvies who built the canals. When canal building slowed in the face of competition, the navvies simply moved across to building railways. By 1850, a quarter of a million workers – a force larger than the British Army and Royal Navy combined – had laid down 5000 km of railway lines across Britain.

Why do the rails seem to end in an earth wall?

How hard was the life of a navvy?

Navvies worked on the railways and slept where they were working. Navvies lived in rough camps, usually far away from shops, pubs or towns. Food quality was poor. Scurvy, a disease caused by a lack of fresh fruit and vegetables, was called the 'railway disease' because so many navvies suffered from it.

Although wages seemed good, navvies had to buy everything from the tommy shop, also called a truck shop. It was a small store that sold tools, clothes, shoes, food and drink – all the things a navvy needed to keep working. The shop, however, was owned by the railway company and it usually charged high prices. During the week, the navvy

Navvies building a railway line.

bought all the things he wanted on credit. On payday he had to pay back what he owed to the tommy shop. The result was that navvies did not keep much of their wages.

Navvies had no official retirement age or state pension, so they worked as long as their physical strength allowed. It was not uncommon to find some navvies doing hard physical work well into their sixties (and remember at this time people aged faster and died younger!).

Was navvy work really dangerous?

Railway lines had to be built fairly level and that meant immense engineering projects. Most locomotives cannot pull loaded carriages up steep slopes and rolling down steep slopes builds up pressure from carriages behind. Metal wheels on metal rails would slip and slide. If a low hill was in the way then a **cutting** was dug. If the hill was too high then a tunnel was dug. If a railway line needed to be raised up above surrounding low-lying land then an **embankment** had to be built. Valleys were crossed by **viaducts** and rivers were crossed by bridges. All these projects cost time, money and lives.

Railways were built mainly by human muscle and horse power. Shovels, pick axes and gunpowder were the normal tools. It was only in the late 1800s that a type of mechanical digger, called the 'steam navvy', became common. Wheelbarrow runs were often feared by navvies. When digging cuttings, vast amounts of material had to be moved. The only way to do this was by pushing wheelbarrows filled with the earth and rocks up steep, slippery runs made from planks of wood. The wheelbarrows were often pulled up by a horse but if the horse pulled too quickly the navvy guiding the barrow could fall from a height and be crushed by falling debris. If the horse slowed or the rope became slack the barrow could topple over with the same danger from falling debris for the navvy.

> ### GLOSSARY
>
> **Cutting** a slice of land cut out of a hill to allow a railway to pass through, avoiding going up and down hills
>
> **Embankment** a raised mound of earth to carry a railway, avoiding going up and down hills
>
> **Viaducts** long bridges supported by arches that carried a railway over low-lying land

This painting shows the viaduct over the River Almond, West Lothian.

Use the internet to search for West Lothian Council's logo. Can you see a connection between the painting and the logo? Look closely, then think why the council chose that logo and what it tells us about the engineering projects of the railway age.

Railway construction was a massive job across Britain – even more so when you remember there was no heavy lifting gear or earth-moving machines. Navvies had to move millions of tons of earth just with their own muscle power. They also had to build the cuttings, embankments and tunnels.

In how many different ways does this picture illustrate the dangers faced by navvies?

A railway cutting in 1837 showing wheelbarrow runs.

Even nowadays, working on railway construction is still not perfectly safe. The Channel Tunnel, Britain's first major new railway for over 100 years, was opened in 1993. It was built by modern navvies who had up-to-date high-tech machinery and good health and safety safeguards. Nevertheless, ten workers died building it between 1987 and 1993.

By the end of the 1800s, the big lines connecting towns and cities had been built but even smaller works on the lines connecting rural areas remained dangerous. Proof lies, for example, on a monument built for the 37 navvies who died during the construction of the West Highland Railway near Arrochar, Tarbet or Ardlui.

Do navvies deserve their bad reputation?

Navvies had a scary reputation as heavy drinkers and hard fighters. When men who had been working in dangerous, tough conditions finally reached a town, they would head for the local pubs and look for the local women. Fights were common and many navvies gained bad reputations. However, the local people knew the navvies were a necessary evil. Without the navvies there would be no railway and without the railway there would be no **prosperity** for the town.

Recent research by historians has found that the bad image of navvies has been exaggerated. In reality they were no different from many other groups of workers trying to survive in hard and dangerous jobs. Many navvies were in fact local workers who had lost their jobs as farm labourers and hoped to make some money while the railway was being built in their area. By 1900, 37,000 km of lines had been built. If the reputation of navvies as being drunken fighters was always true then would so many lines, bridges, cuttings and embankments have been built?

> **GLOSSARY**
> **Prosperity** wealth and good times

Why did some people object to railways?

There was some opposition to railways. Landowners and farmers complained that the countryside would be spoiled, that sparks from the locomotives would set fields on fire and cows' milk would go sour. Some doctors said that to travel at speeds of over 50 km/hour would damage the health of passengers.

The old toll roads had been an improvement in the eighteenth century but with the arrival of the railway there was no need for the coaches or the roadside coaching inns where passengers and horses could rest for the night. Canals and toll roads lost money because of the railways and many of these companies were forced out of business. Landowners who possessed huge country estates objected to railways. They said that trains would bring 'ordinary' people into the countryside and they would just make a mess!

It was clear that those who complained were simply against change, either because they would lose money or would need to change their view of the world.

How did the railways change Britain?

The railways had an enormous effect on the lives of people in Britain. Railways changed the places where people lived in relation to their work and even affected the way in which we tell the time. Trade within the British Isles increased dramatically thanks to the development of the railways. Most importantly, railways transformed the economy of Britain.

What economic benefits did railways bring to Britain?

Railways created jobs

Railways provided thousands of new jobs, from the navvies who built the railways, the bridges and the tunnels, to the ticket collectors, train drivers, firemen, guards, engineers, station masters, ticket clerks, porters, signalmen, catering staff and so on.

Railways boosted industries

To build tracks, carriages and stations, vast supplies of iron, coal, glass and leather were needed. As demand for more coal increased, existing mines were expanded and new mines dug – boosting coalmining. Timber was needed for the construction of the supports to hold the metal rails, but also in the building of carriages. Stations had to be built, employing many craftsmen and labourers. Almost every industry you can think of had some input into the expansion of the railways, and that all generated profit and boosted the British economy.

Railways carried iron sheets and girders from the steelworks in Motherwell and Coatbridge to the shipyards on the Clyde. In the Scottish Borders, the wool industry flourished, while Lockerbie and Newtown St Boswells became important cattle market centres in the Borders. Freshly caught sea fish could be sent from harbours such as Eyemouth, in the Borders, to hotels and shops across Britain. For the first time, fresh produce could be transported quickly to new markets before it started to go off. Fertilisers and coal could be taken to farms.

Local manufacturers could now sell their goods across the whole country, instead of just locally. This led to the expansion of some businesses and the creation of national brands. Cadbury's chocolate, for example, could advertise all over Britain and transport its confectionery anywhere quickly and efficiently. Other brands began to emerge such as Bisto gravy, Bird's custard and Hovis bread. Many of the names we see in the supermarkets today only appeared as a result of the ability to transport goods on the railways.

What social changes did the railways bring to Britain?

The railways led to great social changes. That means railways affected how people lived their lives. Railways allowed towns to grow in size. Better-off workers could escape the noise and pollution of the inner city by moving to suburbs and then commuting back into the city for work. Passengers benefited from quick, cheap travel. Newspapers could be carried all over the country, and not just be about local news. Royal Mail meant that everyone in the country could keep in touch with whoever they wanted much more quickly than before.

Food was cheaper and fresher as it could be delivered quickly to towns. A better diet led to better health for people.

With the new railways came the telegraph system. Along the route of the rail lines, telegraph poles and lines connected cities and businesses across the country. Messages could be sent along the wires quickly and cheaply by Morse code – a series of electronic long and short sounds, called dots and dashes, each pattern of dots and dashes representing a letter. It allowed for almost instant communication and was the first telecommunication system in the world.

Tourism developed as an industry. At first, trips to the countryside for fresh air and exercise were common but soon seaside resorts became popular. Places such as Blackpool and Scarborough offered funfairs and beaches. Huge hotels were built to accommodate the people brought out of the cities by the railways. The British seaside holiday had been invented, where people enjoyed bathing, building sandcastles, eating fish and chips and watching Punch and Judy shows.

Train and steamship journeys allowed Glaswegians to go 'doon the water' in their thousands to holiday on Arran and Bute. In the Lothians, the railways turned Portobello, North Berwick and Dunbar into seaside resorts.

Cheap third-class tickets enabled even working-class people to go on day trips away from the overcrowding and filth of the cities.

> Use Google Images to search for Victorian railway posters. What impression do the posters give about the effects of railways on life in Britain?

A railway company advertising poster.

> Imagine you lived and worked in an industrial city. What does a poster like this tell you about the huge social effect that railways had on people's lives in Britain?

A railway company advertising poster.

The effect of tourism was discussed by the *Chambers' Edinburgh Journal* in 1844:

Not the least important effect is the facilities they have afforded to the humbler classes for recreation. Short trips give the working classes the opportunity of seeing that which they would never have been able under the old stage coach and wagon dynasty. The artisan cooped up and constantly breathing bad air has now the opportunity on every available holiday of making excursions into the country.

> Rewrite this extract in easy-to-understand English.

Did the railways affect sport?

The opening of the Highland railway allowed rich people to travel into the Scottish Highland estates for game shooting, fishing and other outdoor leisure pursuits. This was made fashionable by Queen Victoria, who bought the Balmoral Estate and made regular visits to the Highlands. Railways were also very important in the development of golf. How else would an increasingly urban population get to courses such as St Andrews, Muirfield or Turnberry?

Perhaps the biggest effect on sport by railways was on football. Football had been played in Britain for hundreds of years but the introduction of cheap rail tickets allowed it to become a national game. Fans could follow their teams to rival towns on Saturdays and host matches in return. This led to a more formal organisation of the football game, with registered teams, leagues and cup matches. Queen's Park was the first Scottish football club, officially set up in 1867. The Scottish Football Association was established in 1873.

Did the railways affect politics?

By improving communication, railways allowed news and ideas to spread. People knew about political events taking place across the country. Organisations such as the Chartists and then the Reform League and Union could organise massive demonstrations such as in 1867.

How did the railways change the way in which people kept the time?

Before the railways developed, people had their own time based on the position of the sun in the sky where they lived. This varied from place to place by several minutes. National rail timetables meant that a national time was needed. Railway timetables needed to be co-ordinated with each other so that passengers wouldn't miss their connecting trains. In 1846, Greenwich Mean Time (or GMT) was adopted by all the train companies. That meant everywhere in Britain kept the same time.

> How does this poster capture both the changes in technology and the social changes that railways brought to Victorian Britain?

THE
FLYING SCOTSMAN
1862 - 1962

A railway company advertising poster.

How important were railways to changing Britain?

By 1900, Britain had been transformed. Almost every village in Britain was connected to the rail network. Today, it is still possible to see pubs called the Railway Inn and small roads are called Station Lane even where no railway now exists.

By 1901, any person, no matter where they were, could be linked fairly easily to all of Britain and Britain could come to them with national postal deliveries and national news. In 1896, Janet Foggo sent a postcard from Stenton, East Lothian at 8.30a.m. telling her husband, John, that she would meet him for lunch that day in Princes Street, Edinburgh. John got the postcard at 11a.m. and they met at 12.30. All of Britain was connected and the railways had created a social and economic revolution in Britain.

Activity 1

Summarise this chapter

The following summary reminds you of what this chapter has been about. Words that are important have been made into ANAGRAMS. Your task is to sort out the anagrams and then write the correct version of this summary into your workbook or work file.

Railways started as **CKSTRA** of **LAIRS** on which carts full of **LOAC** rolled downhill to ports. **SESHOR** were used to pull the empty carts back uphill. By the 1830s, **SYWALAIR** started to replace canals. **MOTLOCOIVES** were moving steam engines and they pulled trucks. At first, the railways carried **YHEAV TRIALINDUS** goods such as coal and iron but soon passengers were carried. The first passenger line was between **POOLLIVER** and **CHESTERMAN**. Within the next 20 years, gangs of **VANVIES** worked across Britain building a network of rail lines connecting Britain's towns and industrial areas. Railways provided tens of thousands of new **SBOJ** and changed everything from **BALLFOOT** to **TEDI**.

Activity 2

If this is the answer what is the question?

Below you will find a list of words or names. You have to make up a question that can only be answered by the word on the list. For example, if the word 'Liverpool' was the answer, a question could be 'What was the name of the city that was linked to Manchester by rail in 1830?'

Here is your list of answers:

▶ navvies
▶ Stockton to Darlington
▶ coal
▶ George and Robert Stephenson
▶ Rocket
▶ 1830
▶ wheelbarrow runs
▶ railway time
▶ Portobello, North Berwick and Dunbar.

Activity 3

Picture interpretation

This drawing is part of the decorated top of an old map. The first word is 'Plan'.

▶ In your own words, what do you think that this drawing shows?
▶ In what area of Britain are the places mentioned in the description?
▶ During the Industrial Revolution, which two industries was this area most famous for?
▶ Describe exactly how the illustration shows the early purpose of railways and also how they were operated.

Activity 4

Design a revision mobile

Your mobile should illustrate the development and effects of transport changes between 1760 and 1900. You can choose to work on your own or as part of a group no bigger than four. If you work in a group, you must also design and use a creativity log in which you record exactly what each person in the group contributed to the final mobile.

In practical terms, the best structure is usually two criss-crossing wire coat-hangers.

Here are your success criteria:

▶ Your mobile must have at least four strands.
▶ Two strands should be about canals and two should be about railways.
▶ Each strand should have several mobile items attached.
▶ Each strand must have two text items, perhaps only one significant name or word.
▶ Each strand must have at least one large double-sided illustration linked to an event or a personality.
▶ Each strand must have a three-dimensional feature that represents a major event in that strand.
▶ Your mobile should hang easily.
▶ Your mobile must be able to be read from a distance.
▶ Your mobile must be attractive, colourful and relevant to the project task.

Question practice

National 4

How did transport changes between 1760 and 1900 affect the lives of British people?

Your task is to use the historical information in this chapter and anything else you can discover to design a display or make a presentation about how railways and canals affected British people between 1760 and 1900.

Your display or presentation should show the following:

▶ the main events
▶ the main people
▶ the main effects of railways and canals.

There are a variety of ways you can design this. A few ideas are listed below.

▶ You may wish to create an information poster divided into changes caused by canals and changes caused by railways.

▶ Or, you could present the information in the form of a leaflet, a mindmap or a storyboard that details the story of transport changes between 1760 and 1900.
▶ There may also be an opportunity for you to design a slideshow presentation that can be shared with the class or shown on your school's website for revision.
▶ You can produce your own images or you can print off images from the internet to cut out and stick on your information poster to make a collage.

It is important to remember that you will only be assessed on your historical understanding and not on the artistic qualities of your display or presentation. However, it should be presented in a clear and neat manner to allow your audience to fully understand your main ideas.

National 5

Describe the impact of the growth of the railway network on the British economy. (5 marks)

You need to make five separate points from recall.

You can always gain an additional mark if you bring in more information to back up a point you are making. For example: 'The growth of railways boosted the coal industry [1 mark]. A reliable supply of fuel was needed for the growing number of steam locomotives [1 extra mark].'

Chapter 9 Radical protests

What is this chapter about?

In 1760, Britain was not a democracy but by 1900 changes had taken place that
made the country more democratic, although it was certainly not fully democratic.
The Industrial Revolution caused many changes and protests grew. The government
saw these protests as a dangerous threat that should be stopped. Between 1815 and
1820, the government took very strong action against radical protests, and the two
most famous examples were at St Peter's Field in Manchester in 1819 and the Radical
War in Scotland in 1820.

By the end of this chapter you should be able to:

▶ Describe examples of radical protest, especially St Peter's Field in England and the
Radical War in Scotland.
▶ Explain what caused the radical protests and why the government was so against
them.

What does democracy mean?

In a **democratic system** the adult population chooses who
rules the country and makes the laws. In a democracy, people
also have the right to protest against things that they think are
wrong and should be changed.

> **GLOSSARY**
>
> **Democratic system** where people
> have a vote to select how they will be
> ruled

Why was Britain not a democracy in 1760?

In 1760, Britain was nowhere near being a democracy. Most men and all women had
no right to vote. Power was in the hands of rich male landowners and nothing had
changed in the way Britain was ruled for hundreds of years. Protest was not allowed.
All protestors were thought to be dangerous and should therefore be stopped.

How was Britain governed in 1760?

In 1760, there were two political parties called the Tories and the Whigs. There was not much difference between the two parties. Most Members of Parliament (MPs) were landowning wealthy men who were mainly interested in how much power and money they could get for themselves, their friends and their families. MPs certainly did not see the need for any political changes. In fact, one powerful landowner, Lord Braxfield, said in 1793 that the system of government in Britain was 'the best that ever was since the creation of the world, and it is not possible to make it better'.

Until the middle of the 1800s, very few men and no women had the right to vote in British elections. As far as the government was concerned, it could ignore the population as long as there were no big protests. The problem was that by 1815 protests were increasing.

Why did pressures for change increase in 1815?

In 1815, a long war against France had ended. Unemployed soldiers were looking for jobs. Wartime orders for weapons and equipment had ended. Protests about unemployment and hunger and poverty increased.

By 1815, protestors joined groups that wanted political change such as the right to vote. These groups were called **Radicals**.

> ### GLOSSARY
> **Radicals** people who wanted political reform
> **Reform** political change
> **Luddites** a group who protested against unemployment by destroying machinery

What was a Radical?

Radicals wanted a fairer society and a change in the way Britain was run.

A Radical was someone who supported the **reform** of parliament such as giving the right to vote to all men over the age of 21. Radicals hoped that the government would then listen to the voices of working people protesting about living and employment conditions.

> Think about the long-term reasons for the Luddites' discontent. Why would machine breaking not be the answer to their problems?

This shows Luddites reacting against the things that were changing their lives.

To stop the Radicals issuing posters and newspapers, the government passed laws that were meant to gag, or stop, the Radicals. They were called the Gagging Acts. Research those acts, find out what they did and try to link them to the imagery in this cartoon.

Why was the government against political reform?

The outbreak of the French Revolution in 1789 turned 'reform' into something to be feared by those in power. To understand that reaction you must be aware that the French Revolution had started with protests and demonstrations aimed at getting some political reform but it led directly to the deaths of thousands of wealthy landowners and the execution of the French king and queen. The British government did not want to take any chances of the same thing happening in Britain, so they took strong action against Radicals. The scene was set for conflict in the years after 1815.

How did the government deal with protests after 1815?

The title of this cartoon is 'A Freeborn Englishman'. It was drawn around 1819. Mr Bull owned the building on the left. In cartoons, John Bull is used as a typical Englishman. His house is in ruins, his wife in tears and his dog dead. What does this scene represent? On the right is a debtors' prison. At that time you could be imprisoned for not paying your debts. The crowd in the prison asks for help from the passer-by but he shows his empty pockets. The central figure is the ironic 'Freeborn Englishman'.

There was no police force in 1815 and local authorities relied on **yeomanry**. Yeomanry dressed in fancy uniforms and looked like soldiers. The officers in the yeomanry were usually members of wealthy families who were against any change. Ordinary members of the yeomanry usually depended on their officers in everyday life for their jobs and homes. By 1815, yeomanry were being used to guard against any violent radical demonstrations.

Local authorities also employed spies and *agent provocateurs* to guard against radical protests. *Agent provocateurs* were government agents who provoked trouble. They helped to plan the protest and then reported to the government what was happening. That way, the agents were paid. If there was nothing to report they did not get paid. It was therefore in the interests of the spies to make trouble so they could inform the government what was happening. It is hard to tell if many of the radical protests would have happened without the *agent provocateurs* stirring things up.

> ## GLOSSARY
>
> **Yeomanry** local part-time soldiers who were used to stop radical protests
>
> ***Agent provocateurs*** spies who set up Radicals to protest and then informed the authorities to get a reward

What happened at Spa Fields, London?

The first big protest that threatened to erupt into serious violence happened at Spa Fields in London in 1816.

Cities were crowded places so the public parks – or 'fields' as they were called – were important places for meetings.

It was no accident that large-scale protests happened either near to parliament in London or in regions most affected by industrial change, especially the Glasgow area and the industrial north of England.

The first two big protests both happened in London, at Spa Fields. Thousands of people turned up to hear a very famous radical celebrity of the time called Henry Hunt. He was nicknamed '**Orator**' Hunt because he had a big booming voice and spoke very well to large crowds.

The first Spa Fields meeting, on 15 November 1816, attracted about 10,000 people and passed off peacefully. The purpose of the demonstration was to show support for political reform and to ask for help for the unemployed and poor.

About 20,000 people attended the second demonstration, in December 1816. Once again Henry Hunt spoke but trouble broke out. There is some evidence that a small group of people intended to use the meeting as a cover for an attempted revolution and to seize the nearby Houses of Parliament and the Bank of England. On the other hand, the planned revolution was reported by an *agent provocateur* so no one is really sure if the claim of a plot was true or not.

The fact remains that the army was used to break up the crowd and there was some violence. The events at Spa Fields were enough to convince the government that large protest demonstrations were dangerous and that political protest must be stopped.

Who were the Blanketeers?

In the months that followed the Spa Fields meetings, the government continued to use force against protestors. Early in March 1817, spinners and weavers from Manchester planned to march to London to protest about the new steam-powered looms in factories that were destroying the jobs of hand-loom weavers.

The idea was that the weavers should march in groups of ten, each man with a blanket on his back (which led to the name 'Blanketeers'). They intended to march to London but they did not get far. The government called out troops to break up the marchers by force and the leaders were put in prison.

What happened at St Peter's Field, Manchester?

The most famous protest happened at St Peter's Field, Manchester, in 1819.

Between 1815 and 1819, unemployment continued to rise while the factory system spread, bringing with it hard work in harsh conditions.

Radicals increased their demands for political reform. A radical group called the Manchester Patriotic Union planned a large meeting for 16 August 1819 at St Peter's Field in Manchester. As many as 60,000 demonstrators came from all over the Manchester area to listen to speakers, including Henry Hunt. They had been told to be peaceful and many brought along their children and picnics. The local **magistrates** became worried.

While the demonstrators began assembling in an orderly manner on St Peter's Field, the local magistrates met in a pub in the city to decide what to do if the huge crowd became violent. The magistrates had gathered almost 1000 local yeomanry to deal with any potential riot. About 500 of the yeomanry were mounted on horses.

The meeting began at 1p.m. when Henry Hunt arrived in a carriage to speak to the assembled people.

The magistrates panicked when they heard the cheering and roars as Hunt arrived. The magistrates were worried that they would not be able to control the situation and sent instructions to the yeomanry commanders to ride towards the crowd. The cavalry rode into the field, determined to arrest Henry Hunt and the group leaders, but the people pushed in and around the horses, throwing sticks and rocks at the soldiers. Whether it was a plan or just panic among the yeomanry is not clear but the mounted troops used their **sabres**, hacking at the helpless people all around them.

> ### GLOSSARY
> **Cavalry** soldiers on horseback
> **Sabres** large swords with a curved blade designed for use from horseback

A painting of the St Peter's Field meeting.

> How accurate is this picture of the meeting? Start by considering what is true in the picture and then identify what is an exaggeration or false. How did the artist feel about the meeting at St Peter's Field? How can you tell?

More horses charged into the field from different positions. Ten minutes later, the people had fled, but 11 were left dead, and between 400 and 600 were wounded.

What were the consequences of the 'Peterloo Massacre'?

When many of the people who had attended the meeting returned to work they found that they had lost their jobs because they had been at the protest meeting. Even those who had just gone to hear the speeches had been sacked.

The event was later called Peterloo. Four years earlier, the British cavalry had helped to win the final battle of the Napoleonic War against France at a place called Waterloo. At St Peter's Field, the name Peterloo was a sarcastic comment on the brutal attack of yeomanry on a peaceful demonstration.

Compare the two pictures of cavalry at Waterloo and yeomanry at St Peter's Field. Explain the irony and sarcasm involved in calling the meeting in Manchester 'Peterloo'.

'Scotland for Ever'. The charge of the Scots Greys at Waterloo, 18 June 1815.

What was the Radical War of 1820 in Scotland?

Find out what you can about the Scottish insurrection in 1820 and more precisely what 'Scotland free or a desert' means.

Why did the Radical War happen in Scotland in 1820?

In the early nineteenth century in Scotland, unemployment was increasing and food prices were rising rapidly.

There was already a history of radicalism in Scotland

In 1787, weavers went on strike and met on Glasgow Green. Employers asked for government help to break the strike and six weavers were shot. In Edinburgh in 1792, a protest about lack of political reform and increasing poverty resulted in troops shooting protestors. In 1794, an organisation called Friends of the People campaigned for peaceful political reform. The leaders were arrested and sentenced to 14 years' transportation to Australia. In 1797, a riot in Tranent, East Lothian, where miners refused to be forced into the army, resulted in mounted soldiers charging the crowd and killing 12 people – even more than at Peterloo!

In 1820, discontent about the political system and the spread of steam-powered looms had reached its peak. At the time, only about one in 250 people in Scotland had the right to vote. Many workers in central Scotland, especially weavers, were educated people and they set up societies to discuss how best to campaign for political reform. What followed became known as the Radical War, also known as the Scottish insurrection.

1820 SOCIETY SCOTLAND FREE OR A DESERT

The 1820 Society's protest flag.

In April 1820, a group of men planned to set up a separate government in Scotland and to use force if necessary. Posters were put up all over west-central Scotland urging workers to go on strike and prepare for an armed uprising. It is likely that the posters were put up by an *agent provocateur* but they had the effect the government wanted. About 60,000 people went on strike and troops lined the streets of Glasgow ready for trouble. As tension increased, Radicals organised themselves on Glasgow Green and began training as a 'people's army'.

Meanwhile, Radicals in Lanarkshire collected arms and ammunition. In Strathaven, Radical weaver James Wilson was the central figure planning an armed uprising on 2 April 1820. News reached the Strathaven Radicals of other groups meeting at Cathkin Braes, Glasgow, to prepare for a march into the city to attack government forces. When 50 armed Strathaven Radicals arrived at Cathkin Braes they found no other radical groups had joined them. Instead, government forces were waiting to arrest Wilson.

Next, the remaining Radicals were persuaded, possibly by a government agent, to march to Carron Iron Works, near Falkirk. The works made many guns and cannons for the army and the navy and the Radicals intended to seize those guns and hand them out to the strikers.

But was that really going to happen? The authorities were well aware of what was going on. Government spies reported that trouble was brewing and there is a strong suggestion that *agent provocateurs* 'set up' the protestors. They may even have suggested the march to Carron Iron Works to give the government an excuse to take action against the protestors. The government's plan was simple: allow the conspirators to begin their revolution, then swoop in and arrest them.

In early April 1820 about 40 Radicals marched to seize the Carron Iron Works but soon about half the men had given up and gone home. On 25 April 1820 the remaining Radicals stopped to wait for hoped-for reinforcements and they were met by the Stirlingshire yeomanry and some regular army soldiers. The officer in charge of the soldiers ordered his men to charge the Radicals, who took shelter behind a low wall near the top of a hill. Several shots were fired and the Radicals made good use of their long pikes to keep the horses at bay. Eventually the cavalry made it past a gap in the wall and quickly surrounded the revolutionaries. Four of the radicals were wounded and 19 were arrested. This was later called the Battle of Bonnymuir.

Among the people killed in the Massacre of Tranent was Jackie Crookston, whose statue in Tranent's civic square helps to commemorate the massacre.

What do you think might have happened if the Radicals had got hold of some of these guns?

This is a carronade, a type of small cannon that was made in Carron Iron Works.

> What does this well-kept memorial to an event almost 200 years ago tell us about attitudes towards the Radicals nowadays? How can you explain such attitudes?

What happened to the Radicals?

The leaders of the short-lived rebellion were quickly arrested. James Wilson of Strathaven was executed in Glasgow by hanging, and then beheaded. Two of the Radicals arrested at Bonnymuir, John Baird and Andrew Hardie, were also hanged and beheaded, this time at Stirling Castle. Twenty other Radicals were sentenced to transportation to Australia to serve in the prison colony there for the rest of their lives.

After 1820, the Radical cause seemed to be dead. As the economy improved, new jobs were to be found and there were less desperate cries of protest from the people. However, the ideas of political reform did not die out.

A memorial to the Battle of Bonnymuir.

Activity 1

Summarise this chapter

The following summary reminds you of what this chapter has been about. Words that are important have been made into ANAGRAMS. Your task is to sort out the anagrams and then write the correct version of this summary into your workbook or work file.

In the 1790s, the French Revolution had inspired some **CALRADIS** in Britain that political change was possible. Radicals wanted the **ORMREF** of parliament to give ordinary people a vote. After 1815, hardship and unemployment increased and so did **ICALRAD TESTPRO**. The government was afraid that demands for political change would lead to **UTIONREVOL**.

Activity 2

The challenge! How far can you go?

The following questions go up in level of difficulty in pairs. The first two are easy. The last two are hard. How many will you try to do?

1 Who was Henry Hunt?
2 What did the Radicals want to get?
3 Why did the Radicals think that the answer to question 2 would help their daily lives?
4 Using what you know about political ideas at the time, explain why the government was not likely to listen to Radical demands.

5 Just by looking at the pictures in this chapter, what conclusions can you make about progress towards political reform by 1820?
6 Imagine you are a Radical supporter of reform in Scotland in 1820. Design a one-page handout that will attract attention. Explain why you want reform and what kind of reform you want.

Activity 3

Wordsearch

Make your own larger version of the wordbox shown here. Draw it large enough so that you can write letters in the boxes.

Use the wordsearch grid to hide five main words, names or ideas linked in some way with the Radical War in Scotland in 1820. Complete the grid with random letters to conceal your words. Do not show where the words are on your grid; your partner must find them. So, what you do is write definitions of the words below or beside your wordsearch.

When you have completed your wordsearch puzzle, exchange with your partner. Read their clues and find their words. As they solve your puzzle, you solve theirs.

Question practice

National 4

Source A is from *Waterloo to the Great Exhibition* by Colin McNab and Robert MacKenzie, published in 1982.

SOURCE A

The Radical War broke out in the spring of 1820 when weavers, whose pay had been falling, went on strike. Radical posters were put up on walls in Glasgow calling on people to strike. Only a few workers, led by James Wilson, marched on Glasgow with weapons to try to start a revolution. They found no support there and went home. Wilson was arrested and put on trial.

Describe in your own words some of the things that happened in the Radical War of 1820 in Scotland. You should use Source A and your own knowledge.

Success criteria

Include at least two factual points of information, or one developed piece of information, about what happened in the 1820 Radical War. You can write about the good things and the bad things if you want to.

National 5

Source A is from *Waterloo to the Great Exhibition* by Colin McNab and Robert MacKenzie, published in 1982.

SOURCE A

The Radical War broke out in the spring of 1820, when workers in Glasgow and surrounding towns attempted a rebellion. Many weavers, whose pay had been falling, supported the call to strike. Radical notices were posted in Glasgow calling on people to revolt. Only a few workers actually took up arms. One group of armed Radicals, led by James Wilson, marched on Glasgow. They found no support there and went home. Wilson was arrested and put on trial.

1 Evaluate the usefulness of Source A for investigating the importance of the Radical Movement in Scotland in 1820. You may want to comment on who wrote it, when they wrote it, why they wrote it, what they say or what has been missed out. **(6 marks)**

Success criteria

▶ To get 1 mark, you need to explain the importance of each of the points you make about the source.

▶ Up to 4 marks may be given for evaluative comments about origin and purpose. Comments about the origin may include an explanation about the type of source, the author or the timing of the source. Comments about purpose may include an explanation about why the source was written.

▶ Up to 2 marks may be given for your evaluation of the content of the source which you consider is useful in terms of the proposed question. For full marks to be given, each point needs to be discretely mentioned and its usefulness explained.

▶ If you list information, it will be considered to be one point and will get only 1 mark.

▶ Up to 2 marks may be given for evaluative comments relating to points of information not mentioned in the source.

2 To what extent did the Radicals pose a serious threat to order in Scotland in 1820? **(8 marks)**

If the question starts with 'To what extent' you must write a balanced answer.

In your answer you should show that you understand that the Radicals did pose some threat to order in Scotland. You could write, 'On one hand the radicals did pose a threat because …'. You could mention things such as Radical notices being posted in Glasgow calling on people to revolt. Aim for at least two other pieces of information suggesting the Radicals were a threat.

You should then balance your answer. You could write, 'On the other hand the Radicals were not such a threat because …'. You could mention that the Radical forces involved were too weak to pose any serious threat. Aim for at least two other points of factual information.

Finish with a conclusion giving an overall answer to the question, supported by a reason for the judgement you have made. You could write, 'In conclusion, I think the Radicals were not such a threat because …'.

Chapter 10 The 1832 Reform Act

What is this chapter about?

The Great Reform Act of 1832 was the first change in the way MPs were chosen for almost 200 years. The Reform Act tried to make some changes that recognised the effects of the Industrial Revolution. The act also got rid of many of the confusing rules about who could vote depending on where they lived. However, the 1832 Reform Act disappointed many people because it did not do enough to make Britain more democratic.

By the end of this chapter you should be able to:

▶ Explain why parliament needed to be reformed before 1832.
▶ Describe the changes made by the Reform Act of 1832.

Why was there such discontent with the political system before 1832?

Before 1832 the parliamentary system was **corrupt** and undemocratic. Political power was in the hands of big landowners. However, since the Industrial Revolution, the new middle classes such as factory and mine owners and businessmen challenged the idea that landowners should have so much power. The middle classes argued that they should have a say in running the country because they were the new wealth creators.

> **GLOSSARY**
> **Corrupt** dishonest or crooked

This picture shows reformers trying to cut down a rotten tree representing the corrupt political system. On the other side of the tree are people who do not want to change the system.

Search Google Images for 'Rotten borough tree' to find this cartoon and enlarge it so that you can read all the writing. Find out the meaning of all the words in the cartoon. In small groups, draw a sketch of this cartoon and rewrite the text in your own words so as to be able to explain clearly what each side is wanting. As further research, try to find out who the name 'Grey' refers to.

In what ways was the electoral system so corrupt and unfair?

Another phrase for the voting method is the **electoral system**. People who vote are called electors. The main problem was that the electoral system had been created hundreds of years before and did not represent the social changes caused by the Industrial Revolution.

A cartoon showing what happens when the population changes but parliament doesn't.

Each MP occupied a 'seat' in parliament. The area represented by an MP is called a **constituency**. Nowadays each MP represents roughly the same number of people but back then population changes had made some areas much busier and some areas almost deserted. The **distribution of seats** was very unfair. The drawing above is about the distribution of seats. Up until 1832 there had been no real attempt to make the distribution of seats fairer across the UK.

Over hundreds of years, and especially since 1760, people had moved around Britain looking for work. The **distribution of the population** had altered because of the Industrial Revolution. The result was that some places had become depopulated as people moved away and had only a handful of voters, yet still had the right to send perhaps two MPs to the **House of Commons**. The opposite was also true. Small villages that had no right to send an MP to parliament had now grown into industrial towns such as Manchester (with 60,000 people), Birmingham, Leeds and Glasgow. These cities now had tens of thousands of people but they still had no MPs to represent them in parliament.

GLOSSARY

Electoral system the way MPs are elected

Seat each MP has a seat in parliament so a seat is another way of saying an MP

Constituency the area that an MP represents

Distribution of seats the way the total number of MPs is shared across the country

Distribution of the population how the British population was spread around the country

House of Commons one of the two Houses of Parliament. Its members are MPs (Members of Parliament)

Looking at the overall national distribution of MPs, certain areas of Britain, such as the rural south of England, were over-represented while other areas in the industrial north of England and central Scotland had no **representation** in parliament at all.

One of the depopulated **rotten boroughs** was Old Sarum in Somerset. It had once been a busy hill-top town but by 1800 was almost deserted. Another place that became deserted was Dunwich in Suffolk. The problem with Dunwich was that most of the town had fallen into the sea due to coastal erosion, yet it could still send MPs to parliament.

GLOSSARY

Representation MPs represent the people who vote for them

Rotten boroughs towns that still sent MPs to parliament even though they had few or no inhabitants

Imagine that you were the editor of the magazine. Make a short statement to your reporters explaining why you issued a front page like that. What were you trying to show? What point were you trying to make?

Literacy matters!

The following extract is from a supporter of political reform called Tom Paine. In his book, *Rights of Man*, Paine wrote about rotten boroughs:

The county of Yorkshire, which contains near a million souls, sends two county members; and so does the county of Rutland which contains not a hundredth part of that number. The town of Old Sarum, which contains not three houses, sends two members; and the town of Manchester, which contains upwards of sixty thousand souls, is not admitted to send any. Is there any principle in these things?

Rewrite Tom Paine's sentences in modern everyday language. Here are the first few words to get you started: 'There are almost a million people living in Yorkshire but it only gets to choose two MPs while …'

The Mirror
OF
LITERATURE, AMUSEMENT, AND INSTRUCTION.
No. 492.]　　SATURDAY, JUNE 4, 1831.　　[Price 2*d*.

THREE BOROUGHS

Proposed to be wholly disfranchised by the REFORM BILL.
1. DUNWICH.　　2. OLD SARUM.　　3. BRAMBER.

VOL. XVII.　　2 B

Three places are shown in a magazine, published in 1831, protesting against rotten boroughs.

Elections were corrupt

Before 1832, some of the worst corruption happened in rotten boroughs where powerful landowners or rich businessmen controlled the election result to suit themselves. In some of these rotten boroughs local landlords would often buy the elections for their sons or friends, simply to gain influence in parliament.

Explain why this cartoon was used to illustrate the problem of corrupt elections.

Here they are, all good voters – ready to vote for my coach horse if I order them. Give me the money and I'll secure you the seat.

Well, here's the cash – as for the votes I'll leave them to you.

'How to get made an MP!' A cartoon from 1830.

In these rotten boroughs there were very few voters, so it was very easy to bribe or threaten voters with violence if they didn't vote as they were told. Even where there were many people with the right to vote, corruption was common. Local landowners or rich industrialists could influence the election by threatening their workers with dismissal from their jobs or eviction from their homes unless they voted for a certain candidate. In the countryside, farm workers who had the vote were often threatened with losing their farms if they didn't vote the way their landlords wanted.

The voting system was unfair

All voting was done in public by raising your hand or shouting out who you wanted to vote for. It was therefore easy to know who people voted for. Landowners or factory owners were able to tell if their tenants and workers were following instructions about how to vote. The result of this system of voting was that bribery and intimidation of voters by landowners and businessmen were common.

Why was parliament eventually reformed in 1832?

By 1832, Britain was changing. The growing economy was producing a wealthy middle class who resented being excluded from the political system. They argued that since they produced the wealth of Britain they should have a say in its government.

There was also a growing demand for reform from radical groups and the working class. Politicians argued that if no reform was given then Britain risked a revolution. However, if some reform was given to include the middle class then pressure for reform would be weakened. There had been plenty of protest incidents to worry the government. The radical movements in northern English industrial cities and in Scotland around 1820 had been bad enough, but more radical groups had started appearing in London.

Eventually, some politicians realised that they had to offer at least some reforms to the middle class in the hope of defusing the threat of revolution. One politician at the time, Thomas Macauley, said, 'Reform, that we may preserve.' If 'preserve' means to keep something safe and 'reform' means change, what do you think Macauley meant?

Finally, another reason for reform was because the Whigs took control of the government in 1832. There were two political parties in Britain at that time: the Tories (who were against any reform) and the Whigs (who were prepared to accept some reform).

Describe what you can see. There was no secret voting and voters had to call out the name of the person they wanted to vote for. Why might many voters feel intimidated or threatened if they were trying to vote here?

An election in progress.

What did the 1832 Reform Act change?

After a long struggle in parliament between the Whigs and the Tories, the Reform Act of 1832 became law, with a separate reform act for Scotland in 1833. The new laws did change parliament – but was it enough?

▶ The Reform Act changed the distribution of seats. Sixty-seven new constituencies were created and spread among the industrial areas so that large industrial towns like Manchester had an MP.

▶ Some rotten boroughs lost the right to send MPs to parliament because almost no one lived there anymore. Fifty-six of the most corrupt were abolished and another 30 boroughs were only allowed to send one MP to parliament instead of the two they had sent before 1832.

▶ The act got rid of many confusing and differing rules about who could vote depending on where people lived. It set new rules, which applied across the whole of the UK, based on the value of property owned or rented by voters.

Why did the 1832 Reform Act disappoint so many people?

For many the act did not go far enough. The rules about owning property above a certain value meant that the middle class got the vote but working-class people were still excluded. Out of a population of 14 million there were 13 million people who still could not vote.

▶ Five out of six adult men could not vote.
▶ Women had no right to vote.
▶ There was still no secret ballot, which meant bribery and corruption continued.
▶ MPs still had to own property so only wealthy landowners or businessmen could stand for election.
▶ Country areas, which were controlled by landowners, still had too many MPs.
▶ Many large towns still didn't have any MPs.
▶ MPs were still unpaid, so no working person who relied on earning a wage could be elected even if he owned enough property to qualify for election.

The 1832 Reform Act left many wealthy people happy but many working-class people bitterly disappointed. Since parliament did not look like it would deliver the changes working-class people wanted, they decided that they would have to take action themselves to try to force change. This action for change led to Chartism.

'Merry making.'

Can you explain why the poor were so disappointed by the Reform Act?

Activity 1

Summarise this chapter

The following summary reminds you of what this chapter has been about. Words that are important have been made into ANAGRAMS. Your task is to sort out the anagrams and then write the correct version of this summary into your workbook or work file.

Before 1832, the elections of **PMs** were very unfair. There was no **CRETSE TINGVO** so voters could be **BEDBRI** or **LLIEDBU** into voting for people they were told to vote for. **TENRTO OUGHSBOR** were places where there were hardly any **TERSVO** and MPs were chosen by the local important **OWNRELAND**. The spread of MPs across the country was also unfair and that would only be solved if the number of MPs was evenly **BUTEDREDISTRI** across the country. Ideally more MPs would be given to busy towns and empty areas in the country would have no right to send MP to parliament.

Activity 2

Cartoon interpretation

This cartoon is a sarcastic attack on the political system in Britain before 1832. Can you explain why the cartoonist drew or what he meant by the numbered features? There are clues to help you think about the meaning of the cartoon.

1 The building on the left is called St Stephen's – a reference to the area of London where parliament was. The building is drawn like a mill but instead of producing corn it produces money flowing into the giant tub.

2 The words at the bottom say, 'the system that works so well' – but who does it work well for?

3 Politicians are filling their pockets with money raised from taxation pouring down the chute. Link features 1, 2 and 3 together to explain the artist's opinion about parliament and politicians in 1830.

4 The poor are dumped like waste products under the mill.

5 Weapons – muskets and cannons – hold up the building and the chute. Think about what happened to Radicals who had protested before 1832 and then explain the link between features 4 and 5 and the corruption shown in features 1, 2 and 3. What is the artist suggesting would happen if the poor rose up to protest against political corruption?

Discuss and express your overall opinion of the cartoon. Why did the artist draw this cartoon? Do you think the artist was being accurate and fair in dealing with the political situation in Britain around 1830? Does that matter?

Activity 3

If this is the answer what is the question?

Below you will find a list of words or names. You have to make up a question that can only be answered by the word on the list. For example, if '1832' was the answer, a question could be 'In what year did the Great Reform Act happen?'

Here is your list of answers:

- Old Sarum
- Whigs
- constituency
- rotten borough

- redistribute
- Macauley
- bribery.

Question practice

National 4

Source A is from a speech by Mr Blair Connor, radical leader in Midlothian, 1831.

SOURCE A

Anyone who owns no property cannot vote. Any women, whether she owns property or not, cannot vote. Anyone who tries to vote against the wishes of their landlord or employer risks losing their home and their job for there is no way of hiding who we vote for! This system is wrong. It must be changed.

Describe some of the complaints people had with the voting system before 1832. You should use Source A and your own knowledge.

Success criteria

Include at least two factual points of information, or one developed piece of information, about what was wrong with the voting system before 1832.

National 5

Explain why many people were unhappy with parliament and the voting system by 1830. (5 marks)

You need to make five separate points from recall. To start you off you could mention that voting was not done in secret and the distribution of MPs was unfair.

Chapter 11 The Chartists

What is this chapter about?

The Chartist movement developed out of disappointment with the 1832 Reform Act but the people who supported Chartism had their roots in the radical protests after 1815. 'The Chartists' was just another name for groups of people who wanted the government to listen to their needs. The Chartists were split in how they wanted to achieve their demands and in the short term they seemed to fail. However, in the longer term their ideas lived on to inspire other protest groups. Today, all but one of the Chartist demands are part of our democratic system of government.

By the end of this chapter you should be able to:

- Describe the aims and methods of the Chartists.
- Explain why the Chartist movement grew so quickly and why it declined.
- Decide whether Chartism did or did not fail.

Why did protest grow again after 1832?

The 1832 Reform Act disappointed many people because it did not do enough to make Britain more democratic. Most of the people who benefited from the 1832 Reform Act had been the middle class and industrialists. The ordinary workers were hugely disappointed by the failure to gain the right to vote.

To make matters worse, in 1834 a new **Poor Law** was passed which introduced the hated workhouse system in England and the poorhouse in Scotland. In those places, the poor were treated as if their poverty was their own fault. Only the desperate would to go to these places because conditions inside were kept deliberately harsher than the worst conditions of the poorest person living in their own shelters. Families were split up and children removed from their parents. In the workhouses, the poor had to do horrible, disgusting jobs to earn their food and shelter. The working class was furious. Protest groups gathered across Britain.

> **GLOSSARY**
>
> **Poor Law** an 1834 act to make the poor go into workhouses, where the conditions were very bad
>
> **Laissez-faire** a French phrase meaning to leave alone and not get involved in people's lives

By the mid-1830s, Britain faced another economic recession. Unemployment increased and people feared ending up in workhouses or poorhouses. However, the government believed helping the poor was not its responsibility. This government idea is called *laissez-faire*.

Who or what were the Chartists?

The London Working Men's Association (LWMA) was started in 1836. It was a radical group wanting much greater political reform, especially changes to give the working classes real influence in government. It was the LWMA that issued a six-point 'People's Charter' to make parliament fairer and more democratic. The Charter provided all other radical groups, new and old, with something to aim for. (A charter is just an old-fashioned name for a legal document.) Supporters of the Charter's demands were called Chartists.

What were the six demands?

The Charter's demands for reform were:

1 Universal manhood suffrage – all men to have the vote.
2 Secret voting – to end bribery and corruption at elections.
3 Equal electoral districts – each MP to represent roughly the same number of people.
4 Elections every year – so that MPs could be voted out if they did not keep their promises.
5 No property qualification for MPs – so that people who did not own land could become MPs.
6 Pay for MPs – so that poor men could afford to become MPs.

The Chartist movement grew quickly and it became one of the largest movements of the nineteenth century. The movement began in earnest in 1838 with a series of local radical groups in Glasgow, Birmingham, Manchester and Leeds all organising rallies and marches to support the People's Charter. These radicals soon realised that they needed to work more closely together in order to get anything changed.

What was the national convention of 1839?

The national convention was a group of 50 representatives from different radical movements across the country. The representatives began organising a month-long **general strike** that would hurt the profits of business and might make parliament accept the Chartist demands. The Chartists called the planned strike their sacred month.

The Chartists also planned to get people to sign huge **petitions** in support of the six demands and then present the petitions to parliament. Some members of the convention were so determined to achieve their goals that they were willing to use violence and law breaking. This, of course, alarmed the government, and it refused to listen to the Chartist's petition when it was presented to parliament.

The Chartists presented their petitions to parliament three times in all: in 1839, 1842 and 1848. On each occasion the petitions were rejected.

> **GLOSSARY**
>
> **General strike** where a large proportion of the country's workers stop working
>
> **Petition** a collection of signatures from people to show parliament the high level of support for change

If you were an unemployed worker in Stockport in 1842, what would you have done if you saw the scene shown in this picture? Explain your actions or lack of them.

This drawing shows Stockport workhouse under attack in 1842. The protestors took 672 loaves of bread from the workhouse and handed them out to the hungry poor. Across Britain groups of working-class people joined together to demand more reform.

Faced with such opposition from parliament, the Chartists began to split and argue over how best to get their demands. William Lovett believed that only '**moral force**' (peaceful persuasion) would win through. The Chartist moral force campaigns involved publishing newspapers, posters, petitions and holding public meetings. All over the country there were Chartist churches and Chartist Sunday schools.

Fergus O'Connor believed '**physical force**' (violent uprising) would be necessary. O'Connor even claimed that he wanted to start a national revolution for the working people!

This split in the Chartist movement, and some people talking about using force, made it possible for the government to claim that the Chartists were dangerous revolutionaries. The government nowadays might say the physical force Chartists were like terrorists and this would make it easy to ignore their demands and take forceful action against them.

The hard attitude of the government against the Chartists was shown in 1842 when factory workers in the north of England organised a strike, known as the Plug Plot, in support of the People's Charter. Striking workers removed the plugs from steam engine boilers to bring a stop to production. The machines would not operate without water in the boilers. This hurt the profits of the factory owners and if the idea spread then industry could be seriously damaged. The government reacted as if this was a terrorist campaign. Around 1500 strikers were arrested and sentenced to between 7 and 21 years' transportation to Australia.

In Wales, in the early morning of Monday 4 November 1839, around 5000 workers arrived at Newport. Many of the protestors carried guns and pikes. Were these to be used for attack or defence? The protestors remembered Peterloo and may have been scared of an attack by soldiers. However, there is little doubt that the leaders saw it as a way of starting a Chartist revolution, beginning in Newport and then spreading across industrial Britain. The authorities in Newport were ready for trouble. Troops were waiting to take action and gunfire suddenly broke out. The gun battle went on for the next 25 minutes. At least 22 marchers died, 50 were wounded and two soldiers were seriously hurt.

Three Chartist leaders were arrested and sentenced to be hanged, drawn and quartered. In the end, the execution did not happen for fear that these leaders would be seen as martyrs and cause more trouble in death than they had in life. Instead, the men were sent to prison in Australia. At that time Australia was used by Britain as a place to send all of its serious criminals. The British government hoped that the criminals would never come back.

In reality, the physical force Chartists were more about talk than action, and there was very little Chartist violence.

GLOSSARY

Moral force using peaceful protest methods

Physical force using forceful protest methods

Do you think the artist was for or against the Charter? Use the cartoon and its words to help make your decision.

NOT SO VERY UNREASONABLE! EH?

A cartoon published in 1848.

Is this artist for or against the Chartists? How are they shown? Is this an effective mockery of Chartists? What was the cartoonist trying to achieve when he drew it?

The two cartoons form a pair and they feature the same character. On the left, the man is saying 'Hooray, weeve (we have) liberty! Harm (arm) yourselves!!! To the palis (palace) Down with heaverythink!! (everything)' The right shows the man being arrested by a policeman. 'Oh sir – please sir – It ain't me sir – I'm for "God save the Queen" and "Rule Britannia". Boo – Hoo – oh dear!!' The man then bursts into tears.

How can you tell this is a scene based on the Newport Chartist fight in 1839?

A photograph of a mural in Newport. (This was destroyed in 2013 to make way for a new shopping centre.)

The Chartist movement came to an end in 1848 when the final petition was rejected and troops broke up a Chartist demonstration at Kennington Common in London. The authorities were very well prepared and intended to stop the meeting. In addition to the police and the army, 10,000 special police constables had been recruited, many from the middle class. The government announced that the meeting was banned and only a fraction of the expected number of Chartists turned up. O'Connor urged his followers to go home peacefully and the rally came to nothing.

An early photograph of the Chartist meeting on Kennington Common, 10 April 1848. Parliament rushed through new laws banning large public meetings and making it easier for people to be tried for treason. This made it much harder for the Chartists to organise future protests. After 1848, Chartism became less of a threat to the government and faded away ... or did it?

Why did Chartism fail?

Chartist support varied. In hard times, people supported Chartism but as the economy improved and jobs returned, support for the Charter faded away.

▶ The government refused to talk to the Chartists and rejected their petitions.
▶ Many of the signatures on Chartist petitions were false and made the Chartists a focus of jokes.
▶ Divisions between the moral force Chartists and the physical force Chartists weakened the movement.
▶ Many workers were scared of losing their jobs or being arrested so they ignored Chartist activities.
▶ The Chartist leader, Fergus O'Connor, was incompetent and most of his schemes failed.

Was Chartism really a failure?

It is true to say that the Chartists were not successful in their aim to have their six-point plan accepted, but they were a significant movement at the time. The Chartist movement was the first real organisation of the working-class population in

Describe in detail what this graph tries to show. Is it useful for explaining the rise and fall of Chartism? How might you improve it?

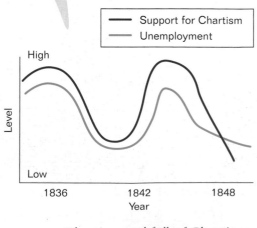

The rise and fall of Chartism.

Britain. In the short term, the Chartists failed but in the longer term their ideas lived on to inspire other protest groups.

The Chartists kept alive the demand for more reform of the election process. Both political parties at the time of the 1832 Reform Act hoped that it was the last reform that the British parliament needed. They were not planning any more. Without the Chartists keeping the issue very much alive it may well have taken longer for any further reform to happen. In the following 60 years, all but one of the Chartist demands became reality.

Activity 1

Summarise this chapter

The following summary reminds you of what this chapter has been about. Words that are important have been made into ANAGRAMS. Your task is to sort out the anagrams and then write the correct version of this summary into your workbook or work file.

Chartism started because many people were very **APPOINTEDDIS** when they got very little from the **REATG RFMORE TCA**. Chartists supported the **EOPLESP TERCHAR** that had **XIS MANDSDE** for **LITICALPO FORMRE**. The Chartists were divided between **RALMO** force Chartists, who believed in peaceful persuasion, and **CISALPHY RCEFO** Chartists, who were prepared to use violence. The Chartist movement faded away but their **DEASI** lived on.

Activity 2

Thinking about cartoons

This cartoon is called 'A physical force Chartist arming for a fight.'

Remember that when the big Chartist meeting was planned for 1848 over 10,000 extra special police constables were recruited to reinforce the police and army. How can you tell this cartoon was drawn when the physical force Chartists were no longer a threat and could be treated as a joke?

Activity 3

Design a storyboard

A storyboard is used to plan a film, so it needs rough drawings showing a main part of the story sequence and any words that you think are necessary – either speech script or scene description. Choose any event or idea from this chapter on Chartism. Research, design, plan and script a storyboard of three frames that tells the story of your chosen subject with accurate detail.

Since you are doing three frames it would be a good idea to work in groups of three or four. Your three frames could be based around why it happened (the *causes*), what happened (the *event*) and what the result was (the *effects*).

Each frame will also need words either as captions or as speech bubbles. Edit your work so it meets the criteria of three frames, captions and accurate detail.

Question practice

National 4

Source A is from Fergus O'Connor, leader of the physical force Chartists.

SOURCE A

I say this! Parliament will only listen to the use of violence to make our point. Hurt its leaders in some way and then they will pay attention to our demands! Big petitions are useless. They can be ignored and made false by government agents filling the lists with false names.

Source B is from William Lovett, leader of the moral force Chartists.

SOURCE B

Violence and threats will get us nowhere. Chartists are people with right on their side and we must persuade our rulers of the justice of our cause. Our petitions will show that thousands support us and parliament must listen to the wishes of the people of this country.

Compare the views in Sources A and B about Chartist protest methods. Describe in detail their similarities and/or differences. You can also briefly compare the overall attitude of the sources.

Success criteria

▶ Examine the two sources in order to show two simple points of comparison or one developed point of similarity or difference.
▶ A simple comparison: 'Source A says … and Source B says …' will get 1 mark.
▶ A developed comparison: 'Sources A and B disagree about the use of violence in Chartist demonstrations. Source A says … and Source B says …' will get you 2 marks.

National 5

SOURCE A

Many working people had supported the 1832 Reform Act in the belief that this would be a first step towards wider democracy. They were angry when the Whig government failed to deliver. In addition, these were hard times; trade was poor, wages were low and faced further cuts and there was fury over the new Poor Law which established the workhouse system. This led to an increased demand for revolutionary change in society that found an outlet in Chartism. This was also a time when, following the repeal [cancelling] of the Combination Acts which had stopped workers forming trade unions, working people were becoming more confident in forming their own organisations.

SOURCE B

The Great Reform Act of 1832 gave the vote to male householders who owned property, which meant that more middle-class men benefited. Only one man in every five had the vote in England and this caused fury among many members of the working class who had expected to be given the vote. Two years later parliament passed the Poor Law Act which introduced the hated workhouses. All those laws seemed to be aimed at hurting the working class. The result was the Chartist movement, which aimed to fight for working-class rights.

Compare the views in Sources A and B of the reasons for the rise of the Chartist movement. (4 marks)

For this type of question you must say whether you think the sources agree or not and then support your decision by making at least two full comparisons using evidence from the sources. You must show links between the sources and not just describe them.

For this question you would probably decide that the two sources agree. You could then back this up with at least two comparisons. You could write something like this: 'Both sources more or less agree about the reasons for the rise of Chartism. One reason was anger at the failure of the Reform Act to deliver democracy. [That is your main point, now what follows is your evidence to back up your point.] Source A mentions working-class anger at the Whig government over the 1832 Act *while Source B also* [this is your link phrase] describes working class fury at continuing restrictions on voting which remained after the Reform Act.'

Now continue your answer by finding another comparison.

Chapter 12 The 1867 Reform Act

What is this chapter about?

By the 1860s, pressure for political change was growing again. Protest groups such as the Reform League and Reform Union organised large-scale demonstrations across the UK demanding more political reform. There were several other reasons why the Second Reform Act was passed in 1867. It is true that many more men were given the right to vote but did the Reform Act of 1867 turn Britain into a democratic country?

By the end of this chapter you should be able to:

▶ Explain why the Second Reform Act of 1867 was passed.
▶ Describe the ways in which the 1867 Reform Act made Britain more democratic.

There was growing support for the idea of more democracy

By the 1860s, pressure for political reform was growing again and there was much less opposition to the idea of change. Politicians who had been powerful in the time of the Radical and Chartist protests were now old men and losing their influence. Prime Minister Lord Palmerston, who had been the main block against any political reform, died in 1865. His death opened the way for new ideas, shown in this letter from a rising star of the Liberal Party, William Gladstone, to Palmerston just before his death in 1864:

My speech cannot I admit be taken for less than a declaration that, when a favourable state of opinion and circumstances shall arise, the working class ought to be enfranchised to some extent as was contemplated in the Reform Bill of 1860.

In pairs, agree on how this letter could be rewritten so that it means exactly the same as the original but is in language that everyone can understand.

Politicians no longer saw the working classes as a violent mob. Skilled working men in cities (called **artisans**) were more educated and respectable. They often attended evening classes and took part in local politics. Politicians accepted that skilled working men were educated and reasonable people who could be trusted with the vote.

National protest groups supported reform

The ideas of the Radicals and Chartists lived on in the national campaign groups of the 1860s. The National Reform Union, based in Manchester, supported giving the vote to respectable artisans and to men who paid a local tax on property, called rates. The Reform League, on the other hand, was far more radical and demanded the vote for all working men. Both organisations were founded in 1864 and increased the pressure for reform.

> **GLOSSARY**
> **Artisans** workers skilled in a particular trade

Do you think the cartoonist believed John Bright? Look at how the cartoonist has drawn the figures and think about how Dr Frankenstein created a monster he could not control. (People who live in Birmingham are sometimes nicknamed Brummies.)

THE BRUMMAGEM FRANKENSTEIN.

This is a cartoon from 1866. The smaller figure is a supporter of reform called John Bright. At a meeting in Birmingham, Bright said he had no fear of supporting universal suffrage (that is, of allowing everyone the vote).

Why do you think this picture has been included in this chapter?

Slaves working on a cotton plantation in the USA.

It might be dangerous to hold back reform

One of the biggest demonstrations supporting reform was in Hyde Park, London, on 23 July 1866. Over 1600 special police constables had tried to prevent protestors from entering the park. However, about 200,000 protestors tore down the railings and flooded in for a massive meeting. Both Liberal and Conservative leaders were very aware that many workers had reached the end of their patience and that the call for reform was supported by workers from every part of Britain. The demonstration was taken as a warning of what might happen if reform was delayed much longer.

World events affected how people felt about political change in Britain

Changes in the USA and Europe helped to build up support for the idea of reform in Britain.

In the USA, the Civil War was fought between the 'North' and the 'South'. It lasted from 1861 until 1865. The war was partly about the use of slaves. The North was the industrial, more modern part of the USA and many of the working- and middle-class people in Britain supported the North. The South was supported by the older landowners in Britain who were against reform.

When the North won the Civil War it was greeted as a sign that the old ways were changing. Many workers in British cotton mills had also taken wage cuts by refusing to handle slave-picked cotton. By not using slave-picked cotton, British workers hurt the economy of the South and helped lead to its defeat and an end to slavery. Many politicians in Britain were impressed by the working-class people who accepted hardship for themselves in order to help other people.

Meanwhile, in Europe, the British government supported revolutions in Germany, Italy and other countries where the middle class was struggling to gain an elected parliament. It would be unfair to support reform abroad yet stop it in Britain.

You might think this image would stop politicians from supporting reform, but how did newspaper drawings like this persuade politicians that reform might actually be necessary?

Protestors pulling down the railings outside Hyde Park in London.

Stealing clothes and winning support!

The two political parties at the time – Liberals and Conservatives – both thought that if they gave the vote to more men then these men would show their gratitude by voting for them.

The Liberals (previously known as Whigs) were led by William Gladstone. When Gladstone suggested a Second Reform Act in 1866 to give more men the right to vote, a row broke out between the Liberals who supported reform and the Liberals who were against it. The Liberals had been the party in government for 20 years but now they split and fell from power. The Conservatives (formerly known as Tories) saw their chance.

Benjamin Disraeli, who became Conservative prime minister in 1868, thought that if his party could pass a reform act of their own, then his party would win more votes. Disraeli also guessed that if the Conservatives did nothing then it was likely that the Liberals would win the next election and the Conservatives would face being out of power for years.

Disraeli acted quickly and stole the Liberal ideas about reform and claimed the Second Reform Act as a Conservative idea! At the time Disraeli's actions were called 'stealing the Liberals' clothes'.

What did the 1867 Reform Act do?

Put simply, more men got the right to vote and the voting system was made fairer.

The right to vote was given to men owning property above a certain value and **lodgers** paying rent above £10 a year. In effect, the vote was given to skilled working men who earned about £1.50 a week – quite a lot at that time. They would have needed that wage to be able to afford to rent the property that qualified for the vote.

> **GLOSSARY**
>
> **Lodgers** people who pay rent to stay in a room of someone else's home

The reform almost doubled the number of men who were entitled to vote. In Glasgow, for example, the number of voters increased from 18,000 to 47,000.

The voting system was made fairer by redistributing seats. The population of Britain was still on the move and as some industrial towns continued to grow, other places became even more depopulated. To make the system fairer, areas that were depopulated lost the right to have an MP while the busier areas gained the right to have MPs representing them. Fifteen towns that had never had an MP now gained one, while Liverpool, Manchester, Birmingham and Leeds each gained an extra MP!

Why could Britain not be called a democracy after the Second Reform Act?

The 1867 Reform Act made Britain *more* democratic but Britain did *not* become a democracy before 1900.

▶ Most men still could not vote. The Reform Act only affected skilled working men in towns. Working men in the countryside could not vote. Men who did not own or rent property up to a value set in the Reform Act had no right to vote. That meant that the poor and unemployed had no vote.

Whose is the face on the horse? Why are other politicians in the background pulling their horses to a halt? If this was a real scene why would the rider be covering her face? Why is Britannia covering her face – in other words, what does the cartoonist feel about the Second Reform Act?

'A Leap in the Dark.' A leap in the dark on horseback is a very dangerous thing to do. Why? The figure on the horse is Britannia. She represents Britain. You can still see her on the reverse of many 50p coins.

▶ The **residency rule** was a new rule that said a man had to have stayed at the same address for at least a year before he got the right to vote. What this meant was that even if the man rented or owned property worth the amount to allow him to vote, he was unable to vote unless he had lived there for at least a year before the election. The residency rule stopped about 30–40 per cent of the male population, who should have had the right to vote, from voting.

▶ After 1867 there was still a lot of corruption. There was no secret voting so it was very easy for **aristocrats** and factory owners to influence elections by bribery or threats. Voters could still lose their homes or jobs if they did not vote the way they were told.

▶ Some men had more than one vote. They were called plural voters. Plural voters were able to vote more than once in a general election. At the time, the right to vote was based on the amount of property owned, so if a person owned property in different constituencies, it meant that he could vote in each one. That meant that richer voters could vote more than once.

▶ No women could vote in national elections, yet they made up half the population. It was not until 1918, after the First World War, that some women gained the right to vote.

GLOSSARY

Residency rule a voter had to be at the same address for a year before being able to vote

Aristocrats very wealthy landowners, usually with titles such as Lord or Duke

- The redistribution of MPs attempted to make a fairer spread of MPs across the country. However, the system was not yet fair, with landowning interests in the south of England still over-represented in parliament while the growing towns were still comparatively under-represented.
- Finally, voters still only had a choice of two, very similar parties. Both the Conservative and Liberal Parties represented old values and the control of government was still in the hands of wealthy landowners. So no matter what party won an election, there was not going to be much change in the lives of ordinary voters.

What happened between 1867 and 1900 to make Britain even more democratic?

In 1872, the Secret Ballot Act was passed. Now people's votes were private and that was a big step forward in reducing corruption in British politics.

The Corrupt Practices Act of 1883 made it illegal to bribe or influence voters in any way so, for example, political parties had a limit on how much money they could spend on elections to impress voters.

The Third Reform Act of 1884 gave the vote to workers in the countryside on the same rules as voters in the towns. Now all adult males owning or renting land worth £10 a year could vote.

In 1885, the Redistribution of Seats Act reorganised constituencies across Britain so that each MP represented roughly the same number of people.

How democratic was Britain by 1900?

In 1900, Britain was still far from being a democratic country. Many men who did not live in property up to a certain value did not have a vote. The political system was still highly dominated by class. The skilled working class could now vote but they only had a choice of wealthy candidates to vote for. Even less democratic, the poor and unemployed had no vote at all so they had no way of influencing the decisions that affected them the most.

Finally, there was the power of the **House of Lords**. The British parliament is made up of two parts called houses. The first is the House of Commons that contains all the elected MPs. The second is called the House of Lords. In 1900, members of the House of Lords were hugely powerful landowners and were not elected. The House of Lords had the power to veto or block anything the elected House of Commons tried to do, so any law passed by MPs in the House of Commons could be vetoed by the unelected House of Lords. Power therefore was still in the hands of the big wealthy landowners who had always influenced government. Britain in 1900 still had a long way to go before it could be called democratic – and, since the House of Lords is still unelected today, maybe still has!

> **GLOSSARY**
>
> **House of Lords** one of the two Houses of Parliament. Its members are unelected

Activity 1

Devise a timeline for your revision

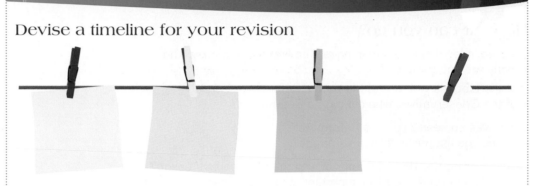

This task is called the British Timeline Washing Line. Your challenge is to make a series of washing lines to hang around your classroom or corridors. The purpose of this task is to revise the entire course you have completed on Changing Britain 1760–1900.

Your teacher will divide the class into groups dealing with the different washing lines. You will need four long washing lines. You decide how long they must be. Each washing line represents a main theme in this section. There are four. Remind yourself of what they are. You will need several pieces of coloured A4 paper. Decide which colour of paper all your material will be written on.

Each theme has two main sections, for example, 'Transport' was divided into canals and railways.

Your job is to select important developments or names or events or ideas in the topic you have been asked to prepare. Use a page of A4 for each event you want to include. Write in large letters so they can be seen and don't write too much on one page.

Now arrange the pages on your topic in date order, starting as near to 1760 as possible. You now need a selection of coloured clothes pegs.

Once your have tied up your washing line, hang out your washing using a peg to place each piece of 'washing' (each event you have written about) on the line – remember to put them in date order.

At the same time as you are doing your washing line, other class groups are doing the same thing for all the other sections in this course – but using different coloured paper.

Once it's all done remember to photograph the lines of washing to help your revision!

Here is a list of things you should be clear about before you start:

▶ You should work in groups of four or five but who is going to do what? You should allocate tasks and responsibilities to ensure all the course is covered.
▶ What text will you use?
▶ What visuals will you use?
▶ How big will this timeline be?
▶ How big should the writing be?
▶ Should this be a small or large group task?
▶ How long will it take?
▶ What resources will you need?
▶ How long do you have to complete it?
▶ Plan to fit in with the time and resource demands.

Activity 2

The challenge! How far can you go?

The following questions go up in level of difficulty in pairs. The first two are easy. The last two are hard. How many will you try to do?

1 Who was the leader of the Liberals who wanted to pass a Reform Act?
2 Who was the leader of the Conservatives who did pass a Reform Act?

3 Why were the Conservatives so keen to pass a Reform Act?
4 Why were many politicians against universal male suffrage?

5 Which of the reasons for passing the 1867 Reform Act was the most selfish reason?
6 Do you agree that the 1867 Reform Act was an important step on the road to democracy in Britain?

7 If you had been prime minister in 1867, would you have wanted to extend the vote to more people? If so, why and to whom? If not, why not?
8 Is it enough to say that democracy means giving people the right to vote? For example, if there was only one party to vote for, would that be democratic? How would you define a democratic country?

Question practice

National 4

Give reasons to explain why the Second Reform Act was passed in 1867.

Success criteria

Write an answer that provides at least two reasons to explain why the Reform Act of 1867 was passed.

National 5

1 Explain the reasons why more people gained the vote by 1867. (6 marks)

To be successful you should try to give five or six different reasons based on recall that must be relevant and accurate. You can always get an additional mark by developing a reason you give. That means you give extra detail to support the point you are making, for example, 'One reason was that politicians felt the skilled working class were more responsible now and deserved the vote [1 mark]. One event that made the working class seem more responsible was when some of the cotton workers took a wage cut rather than use cotton picked by slaves.'

2 To what extent did Britain become democratic between 1760 and 1900? (8 marks)

To be successful in this type of question you must include at least six pieces of accurate and relevant detail and organise them into a balanced answer. You must then give a short conclusion which sums up your answer to the question.

In this question you should show that you understand what democracy means and what was done to make Britain more democratic between 1760 and 1900. You could write, 'Democracy means that all adults in a country have the right to vote freely and fairly and between 1760 and 1900 more people did get the right to vote. In detail …'. You could mention things such as the Great Reform Act and Second Reform Act, who gained the vote and how elections were made fairer.

You should then balance your answer. You could write, 'On the other hand, Britain was not democratic by 1900 because …'. You could mention that women did not have the vote and then give two other reasons why Britain could not be called democratic by 1900.

Finish with a conclusion giving an overall answer to the question supported by a reason for the judgement you have made. You could write, 'In conclusion, I think Britain was more democratic in 1900 than it had been in 1760 but was not fully a democracy because …'.

Glossary

A

Agent provocateurs – spies who set up Radicals to protest and then informed the authorities to get a reward

Agricultural Revolution – agricultural means things to do with farming; revolution means a big change

Anomaly – something odd that does not fit into a pattern. It stands out as different

Aqueducts – water-filled bridges that allow boats to pass over valleys

Aristocrats – very wealthy landowners, usually with titles such as Lord or Duke

Artisans – workers skilled in a particular trade

B

Barges – long flat-bottomed boats pulled along canals by horses

C

Canal mania – a craze to invest money in building new canals, hoping to make big profits

Cavalry – soldiers on horseback

Choke damp – a mixture of gases that remove oxygen from the air

Coastal shipping – ships that carried goods between coastal towns and on main rivers

Competency – the ability to do something properly

Constituency – the area that an MP represents

Contaminated water – water that is polluted by poisons or dirt

Co-operative – a non-profit business run for the benefit of those using its services

Corrupt – dishonest or crooked

Cutting – a slice of land cut out of a hill to allow a railway to pass through, avoiding going up and down hills

D

Death rate – the number of people dying as a proportion of the entire population

Democratic system – where people have a vote to select how they will be ruled

Depopulated – becoming emptier as people move away from an area

Distribution of seats – the way the total number of MPs is shared across the country

Distribution of the population – how the British population is spread around the country

E

Electoral system – the way MPs are elected

Embankment – a raised mound of earth to carry a railway, avoiding going up and down hills

Entrepreneurs – businesspeople who invest their money in new businesses, hoping to make a profit

F

Factories – large buildings containing many large machines operated by many people

Fire damp – an explosive gas

Fragile – easily broken

G

General strike – where a large proportion of the country's workers stop working

H

House of Commons – one of the two Houses of Parliament. Its members are MPs (Members of Parliament)

House of Lords – one of the two Houses of Parliament. Its members are unelected

Hygiene – keeping things clean

I

Incentive – a reason for doing something

Industrial Revolution – the huge change in manufacturing that started about 1760

Industrialisation – a time when society changed from farming to manufacturing

Inspector – a person who had the job of checking that mines were following the law

L

Laissez-faire – a French phrase meaning to leave alone and not get involved in people's lives

Locks – a way of raising barges up and down a series of 'steps' to allow canal traffic to cope with hilly ground

Locomotive – a steam engine that moves under its own power

Lodgers – people who pay rent to stay in a room of someone else's home

Lodging houses – rooms occupied by many people who paid a small rent. Usually worse than slums

Luddites – a group who protested against unemployment by destroying machinery

M

Magistrates – local people who act as part-time judges

Mechanisation – using machines, instead of people making things by hand

Medical advances – improvements in medical knowledge

Migration – the movement of people, either abroad, which is emigration, or to another place within the same country

Mills – usually factories for making textiles such as cotton cloth

Moral force – using peaceful protest methods

N

Narrowboats – self-powered boats for use on canals, similar to barges

Navvies – the labourers who built canals

O

Orator – a speechmaker

P

Pestilent – likely to cause illness or disease

Petition – a collection of signatures from people to show parliament the high level of support for change

Physical force – using forceful protest methods

Pit – a coal mine

Poor Law – an 1834 act to make the poor go into workhouses, where the conditions were very bad

Population distribution – how the population is spread across the country. Sometimes some areas grow as other areas become emptier

Precedent – a guide for future action

Prop – a beam or support to hold something up

Prosperity – wealth and good times

Public health – keeping public areas clean and healthy so that disease does not spread among the population

Pull reason – something that makes people want to move and attracts them to a different place

Push reason – a reason that forces people to move, such as hunger or unemployment

R

Radicals – people who wanted political reform

Reform – political change

Representation – MPs represent the people who vote for them

Residency rule – a voter had to be at the same address for a year before being able to vote

Rotten boroughs – towns that still sent MPs to parliament even though they had few or no inhabitants

Royal Commission – an investigation set up by the government

S

Sabres – large swords with a curved blade designed for use from horseback

Seam – a layer of underground coal that miners cut into

Seat – each MP has a seat in parliament so a seat is another way of saying an MP

Sewage – human faeces and waste

Sewerage – drains and pipes (sewers) to take away sewage

Shuttle – a device for carrying thread or yarn from side to side across a loom

Slums – very poor-quality housing, overcrowded and lacking fresh water or toilets

Spinners – people who spin fibres into long threads or yarn

T

Textiles – a general word for different types of cloth

Tolls – money charged to use a road or canal

V

Ventilation – getting air into the mine to allow miners to breathe

Viaducts – long bridges supported by arches that carry a railway over low-lying land

Villas – detached houses with gardens in middle-class suburbs

W

Weavers – people who make cloth on a loom

Y

Yeomanry – local part-time soldiers who were used to stop radical protests